AN UNOFFICIAL GUIDE TO
BATTLE ROYALE

ALL-TERRAIN SURVIVAL FOR FORTNITERS

MASTER COMBAT SERIES #3

JASON R. RICH

Sky Pony Press
New York

Sky Pony Press books may be purchased in bulk at special discounts for sales promotion, corporate gifts, fund-raising, or educational purposes. Special editions can also be created to specifications. For details, contact the Special Sales Department, Sky Pony Press, 307 West 36th Street, 11th Floor, New York, NY 10018 or info@skyhorsepublishing.com.

Sky Pony® is a registered trademark of Skyhorse Publishing, Inc.®, a Delaware corporation.

Visit our website at www.skyponypress.com.

10 9 8 7 6 5 4 3 2 1

Library of Congress Cataloging-in-Publication Data is available on file.

Cover design by Brian Peterson
Cover artwork by Getty Images

Interior photography by Jason R. Rich

Print ISBN: 978-1-5107-4973-3
E-Book ISBN: 978-1-5107-4978-8

Printed in China

TABLE OF CONTENTS

SECTION 1

WHAT YOU SHOULD KNOW BEFORE GETTING STARTED

What do more than 150 million gamers from around the world have in common? Well, they all play *Fortnite: Battle Royale* on their PC, Mac, PlayStation 4, Xbox One, Nintendo Switch, iPhone, iPad, or Android-based mobile device. These people all love the thrill of exploring the mysterious island, defeating their enemies, and doing whatever it takes to survive.

Are you one of these gamers? If so, by reading this unofficial strategy guide, you'll quickly learn all about the mysterious island where each match takes place, plus learn how to use the island's different types of terrain and climates to your utmost advantage.

As you explore the mysterious island, you'll encounter different climates within the various types of terrain. For example, you may find yourself traveling through snow-covered mountains and over ice-covered lakes, making your way through a network of lava flows, or confronting enemies in a lush forest or urban setting that's filled with paved roads and tall buildings.

Like all combat-oriented "battle royale" games, Fortnite: Battle Royale forces gamers to simultaneously and successfully juggle a wide range of responsibilities. You'll need to fight, avoid the deadly storm, build structures, manage and use your arsenal, and safely explore your surroundings during every match you participate in.

Each type of climate or terrain will force you to contend with a different set of challenges, in addition to the deadly storm and whatever mayhem enemy soldiers try to bestow upon you. Knowing as much as possible about the island and how to use the various types of terrain to your tactical and defensive advantage will be a huge advantage to you.

If your soldier is walking or running over an ice-covered lake, for example, their feet will quickly freeze, and they'll begin sliding rather quickly across flat terrain. You'll have less precise control over your soldier's movements, but they'll travel faster by sliding around.

While ice-covered terrain can be used to your advantage, lava-covered terrain can be deadly. For every second your soldier touches the boiling lava, some of their Health will be depleted. Too much exposure to lava can be deadly.

During each gaming season, different climate and terrain types are introduced onto the island, so it's important to know what to expect, based on where on the island you find yourself at any given moment.

Each time a match begins, your primary goal is to control your soldier and help him (or her) become the last person alive on the island to achieve **#1 Victory Royale**. This applies regardless of which game play mode you're experiencing.

What makes this ultimate objective a bit tricky is that in addition to the game controlling some of the challenges you'll continuously encounter (such as the deadly storm), during each Solo, Duos, or Squads match you'll also need to contend with up to 99 other gamers—in real time—each of whom want to survive and achieve victory just as much as you.

Some of your adversaries will be newbs and pose little threat. Others, however, will have already invested countless hours into perfecting their *Fortnite: Battle Royale* gaming skills. These gamers will have already honed their muscle memory related to the game, perfectly tweaked their game's settings (based on the equipment they're using, their game play style, and their experience level), and are already familiar with the island's diverse terrain. It's these gamers who pose the biggest threat to your soldier's survival.

How to Download and Install the Game

Fortnite: Battle Royale *is a free game. Anyone can download it and start playing on their Internet-connected gaming system without spending a penny. If you're a PC or Mac gamer, to get started, launch your favorite web browser, visit* **www.fortnite.com***, and then click on the Get Fortnite button.*

From your gaming console, visit the online store for your system. From the system itself, PlayStation 4 gamers should visit the PlayStation Store. Xbox One gamers should visit the Microsoft Store, and Nintendo Switch players should visit Nintendo's eStore. Within the store's Search field, enter "Fortnite" to find and download the *Fortnite: Battle Royale* game. (To play on an Xbox One, you'll need to be a paid subscriber to the Xbox Live Gold service.)

Regardless of which gaming system you use, the first time you play Fortnite: Battle Royale *you'll need to set up a free Epic Games account, and potentially link it to your existing gaming system account. For information on how to do this, visit:* https://accounts. epicgames.com/register.

To play Fortnite: Battle Royale *on an iPhone or iPad, launch the App Store, and within the Search field, enter "Fortnite." From the game's listing, tap on the Get button. The Android version of the game is not available from the Google Play Store. Instead, to download and install the game, from your mobile device, visit* **www.fortnite.com/android** *and follow the on-screen prompts.*

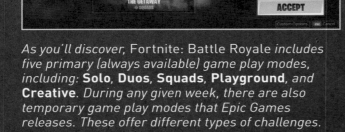

Keep in mind, there's a difference between Fortnite: Battle Royale *(This is also a game title which is a free, combat royale-style game) and* Fortnite: Save the World *(which is a player versus environment game with an intricate storyline). At least initially, the Save the World game needed to be purchased. However, Epic Games announced it will be making this version of the game free as well, most likely sometime in 2019.*

As you'll discover, Fortnite: Battle Royale *includes five primary (always available) game play modes, including:* **Solo***,* **Duos***,* **Squads***,* **Playground***, and* **Creative***. During any given week, there are also temporary game play modes that Epic Games releases. These offer different types of challenges.*

A **Solo** match allows you to control one male or female soldier who must outlive and defeat up to 99 other soldiers on the island (each controlled in real time by a separate gamer) in order to achieve #1 Victory Royale. There's no second or third place. You either win a match, or your soldier perishes.

During a **Duos** match, you'll team up with one other player—either an online friend or someone randomly selected for you. The two of you must work together to defeat up to 49 other two-person teams (98 other gamers) during each match.

When playing a **Squads** match, your soldier will be matched with up to three other soldiers (each controlled by a different gamer). You can choose your squad mates from your online friends, or have the game randomly select the gamers you'll be teamed up with. The four of you, while each controlling your own soldier, must work together to outlive the 24 other squads in the match in order to achieve #1 Victory Royale.

After choosing a Duos or Squads match, select the **Fill** *option if you want the game to randomly select a partner or squad mates for you.*

If you want to choose your own partner or squad mates yourself, select the **Don't Fill** option after choosing a game play mode, and then return to the Lobby.

From the Lobby, select one of the "+" icons located near the center of the screen (to the left or right of your soldier) to invite one online friend at a time to join your upcoming match.

From the displayed list of online friends, select one at a time to be your partner or squad mate.

Choose the Join Party option for the selected gamer. They'll receive an on-screen invitation asking them to be your partner or squad mate for the upcoming match.

The yellow banner that says [Username] Invited You that's displayed above the "+" icon represents an incoming invitation from an online friend who is inviting you to join a match (party).

In addition to inviting friends to join a match and being able to accept invitations sent by others, from the Lobby you can access a wide range of other game-related options by selecting one of the tabs displayed along the top of the screen, or by selecting the game's menu option.

The temporary matches Epic Games offers are sometimes 50v50, team-oriented matches. These involve 100 gamers being divided into two teams. You and your teammates must then work together to achieve specific objectives, which are typically combat related. The Team Rumble Squads mode is an example of a 50v50 match.

Other things you can do from the Lobby include choosing a desired game play mode prior to each match, or viewing a current list of Challenges you can complete during a match. Click on the News button to discover what's new in the game, or at any time, visit **www.fortnite.com/news** *to read the latest Patch notes related to the most recent game update.*

If Epic Games has an important announcement for gamers, a message will be displayed near the bottom-center of the Lobby screen.

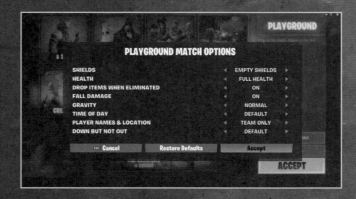

Playground *mode allows you to experience matches created by other gamers. During these matches, it's the person who created the match who chooses the rules of engagement.*

Meanwhile, if you want to custom design the entire island from scratch, and then create your own matches for yourself and others to experience, you'll definitely want to check out Fortnite: Battle Royale's **Creative** *mode.*

To create your own island, select the Creative mode, and then choose the Start A Server option by scrolling to the extreme right. Otherwise, choose one of the showcased modes created by other gamers by selecting one of the listed servers. The selection of showcased custom mode options changes daily.

Regardless of the type of match you choose to experience, each one takes place on the mysterious island which contains at least 20 labeled points of interest (locations), as well as many other regions you'll need to explore. Each area of the map features a different climate and different type of terrain.

To achieve victory when playing *Fortnite: Battle Royale*, it's absolutely essential that you get to know your way around the island and develop a thorough understanding about how to use the different terrain types to your tactical advantage and to help you survive. While this is just one important element of the game, it's the primary focus of this unofficial strategy guide.

Other strategy guides in the unofficial *Fortnite: Battle Royale* Master Combat series (written by Jason R. Rich and published by Sky Pony Press) focus on helping you master other aspects of the game, like how to become an expert marksman using the various guns and weapons offered in the game, or how to travel around the island safely and use the various vehicles and transportation options to your utmost advantage.

To learn more about these other guides, visit **www.FortniteGameBooks.com**.

Don't Judge Soldiers by Their Appearance

Fortnite: Battle Royale newbs (beginners) initially have very few options when it comes to customizing the appearance of their soldier, unless they're willing to spend real money to purchase Outfits and related accessories. Otherwise, it takes time and experience to complete challenges and unlock cosmetic items used to alter a soldier's appearance.

When you encounter an enemy on the island and they are wearing a basic outfit, with no fancy accessories, this can mean one of two things. Potentially, the enemy you're looking at is being controlled by a newb, and that soldier will likely be very easy to defeat.

However, it could also mean that a highly experienced and skilled gamer is disguising their soldier in a basic outfit to make other gamers think they are new to the game in order to give their adversaries a false sense of security before a firefight.

Each of these is an optional outfit that's previously been purchased or unlocked, and that's currently stored within the Locker. To access the Locker, return to the Lobby and click on the Locker tab that's displayed near the top-center of the screen.

If you encounter a soldier who is wearing one of the many limited edition, Legendary Outfits that have been released by Epic Games, and that soldier is also equipped with Legendary Back Bling and an equally unique Harvesting Tool, for example, this too can mean one of two things.

You might assume you're confronting a highly skilled gamer and think twice before engaging them in a firefight. But this could also mean that a newb has chosen to spend some money to customize the appearance of their soldier by purchasing expensive items from the game's Item Shop. In this case, the Sunbird outfit is about to be purchased for 1,200 V-Bucks, which is approximately $12.00 (US).

It's important to understand that the outfit, Back Bling design, Harvesting Tool design, Wraps, and Emotes that you equip your soldier with are for cosmetic purposes only. Regardless of a soldier's appearance, they all have identical capabilities during a match. What sets each soldier apart in terms of what they can do during a match is the skill, experience, cunningness, speed, and creativity of the gamer who controls their soldier.

Ways to Customize the Game Before Each Match

There are several ways to customize the appearance of your soldier, but more importantly, fine tune the gaming controls and audio options so the game is more responsive to your personal gaming style, based on the equipment you're using.

By default, if you're playing *Fortnite: Battle Royale* using a PC or Mac, your primary gaming controls are your computer's keyboard and mouse. Using good quality headphones is also highly recommended, since sound effects are such an important element within the game.

Some serious gamers opt to upgrade their computer hardware with a specialized gaming keyboard and mouse (for added precision and faster response time), plus use a gaming headset (with a built-in microphone) in order to hear the game's sound effects and be able to speak with their partner or squad mates. Another option for computer gamers is to use a gaming controller (sold separately) instead of a keyboard and mouse combo.

Gaming headsets have a built-in microphone. This type of optional accessory is available from a wide range of manufacturers. Some of the more popular gaming headsets used by top-ranked Fortnite: Battle Royale *gamers come from companies like Logitech G (www.logitechg.com), HyperX (www.hyperxgaming.com/us/headsets), Razer (www.razer.com/gaming-headsets-and-audio), and Turtle Beach Corp. (www.turtlebeach.com). Shown here is the HyperX Cloud Alpha headset ($99.99). It's compatible with PCs, Macs, and all popular console-based gaming systems.*

For some gamers, a keyboard/mouse combo offers the most precise and responsive control options, especially if you're using a specialty gaming keyboard and mouse, such as those offered by Corsair (www.corsair.com), Logitech (www.logitechg.com), Razer www.razer.com/gaming-keyboards), and HyperX Gaming (www.hyperxgaming.com). The HyperX Alloy Elite RGB keyboard ($139.99 US) is shown here.

Several companies, including Razer (www.razer.com/gaming-keyboards), offer one-handed, reduced-size gaming keyboards that feature fewer keys than a traditional keyboard, making it easier to reach only the keys needed to play a specific game, such as Fortnite: Battle Royale.

The Razer Orbweaver Chroma, for example, is priced at $129.99 (US). In addition to awesome LED colored lighting effects, it offers 30 programmable keys (which includes 20 programable mechanical keys). Priced at $34.95, the Fist Wizard One-Handed Gaming Keyboard (https://groovythingstobuy.com/products/fist-wizard-one-handed-gaming-keyboard-1) is a less-expensive alternative.

The PS4, Xbox One, and Nintendo Switch versions of *Fortnite: Battle Royale* are designed to be played using the wireless controller(s) that came bundled with your gaming system. For an added edge when it comes to precision and improved response time, consider upgrading your controller to one designed specifically for pro gamers.

Offering more precision than a standard console controller, several companies, such as SCUF Gaming (www.scufgaming.com), manufacture specialty Xbox One and PS4 controllers designed to cater to the needs of advanced gamers. The SCUF Impact controller for the PS4 ($139.95 US) is shown here. These controllers can also be used with a PC or Mac when playing Fortnite: Battle Royale.

It's also possible to connect a gaming keyboard and mouse directly to a console-based system, such as the Xbox One or PS4. The Turret for Xbox One gaming keyboard and mouse ($249.99 US) from Razer is shown here.

If you'll be experiencing Fortnite: Battle Royale *on a Nintendo Switch gaming system, you'll have greater control over your soldier during matches if you upgrade to the Nintendo Switch Pro Controller ($69.99), as opposed to using the Joy-Con controllers that come bundled with the system. More creative gamers have figured out ways to connect a computer keyboard and mouse to a Nintendo Switch (while using the Dock and playing* Fortnite: Battle Royale*). You'll find directions for how to do this on YouTube.*

Regardless of the gaming hardware you're using, memorize the controls for *Fortnite: Battle Royale* and keep practicing using those controls so you develop your muscle memory for the game. When you're able to rely on your muscle memory, you'll be able to react faster without having to think about which key or button to press to accomplish specific tasks.

If you're playing Fortnite: Battle Royale *using a controller on any platform, after accessing the game's Settings menu, select the Controller submenu to customize the controller layout you'll be using to play. The pre-created controller layouts include: Old School, Quick Builder, Combat Pro, and Builder Pro. On most gaming systems, there's also a Custom option that allows you to personalize a controller's*

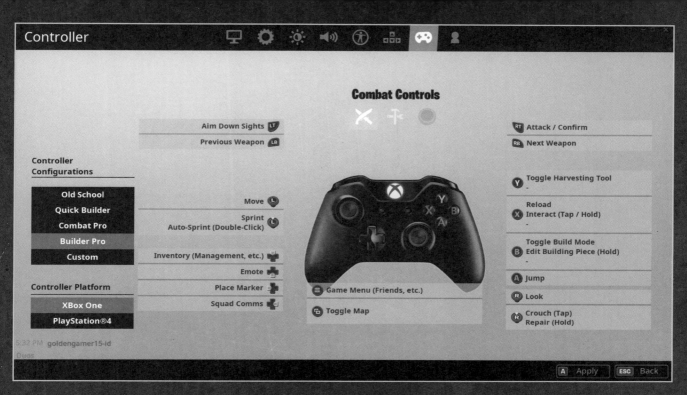

If you choose to connect an Xbox One or PlayStation 4 controller to your Windows PC, for example, from the Fortnite: Battle Royale Settings menu, select the Controller option. Choose your favorite Controller Configuration, and then select between an Xbox One or PS4 Controller layout from the buttons displayed near the bottom-left corner of the screen.

Access the Settings Menu to Adjust In-Game Controls and Options

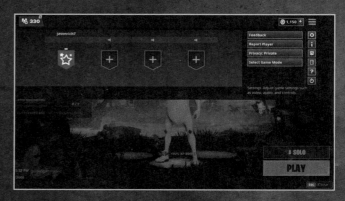

Click on the gear-shaped Settings menu option.

If you're a newb, there are some options available from the game's Settings menu that you might want to adjust. To access the Settings menu, from the Lobby screen (shown here on a PC), select the Menu icon (which looks like three horizontal lines). It's displayed in the top-right corner.

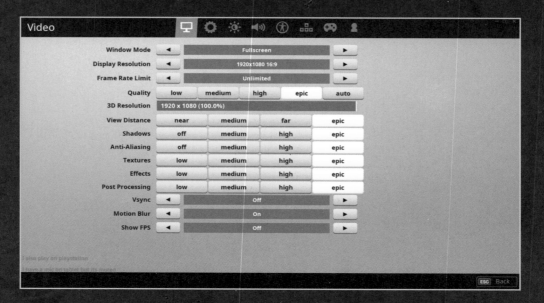

Depending on which gaming platform you're using, a different selection of Settings-related submenu icons is displayed along the top-center of the screen. These include: **Video** *(PC/Mac only),* **Game**, **Brightness**, **Audio**, **Accessibility**, **Input**, **Controller**, *and* **Account**. *The* **Video** *submenu is shown here.*

To ensure the fastest response time from the game, based on the graphics being generated and displayed, from the Video submenu (shown here on a PC), adjust options like Display Resolution, Frame Rate Limit, and Quality. If you're using a lower-end computer that doesn't have a cutting-edge graphics card, for example, you may need to reduce some of these graphics-related options to optimize game play speed.

Based on your gaming experience and game play style, as well as the hardware you're using, from the Game submenu (shown here on a PC), you may want to tinker with some of the settings below the Input heading in order to increase or decrease the mouse's sensitivity, which has a direct correlation to your aiming capabilities and precision when moving your soldier around, for example.

Game

Matchmaking Region	◄	Auto (27ms)	►

Input

Wireless Controller Sensitivity X	0.500	
Wireless Controller Sensitivity Y	0.500	
Wireless Controller Targeting Sen	0.503	
Wireless Controller Scope Sensitiv	0.497	
ess Controller Building Sensitivity	1.000	
Invert View	◄ Off ►	
Invert Aircraft Controls	◄ On ►	

Camera and Display

Anonymous Mode	◄ On ►	

🎙 Hold to chat   ⬜ Reset   ◯ Back

The same menu is shown here on a PS4. (A similar menu is offered within the Xbox One and Nintendo Switch version of the game.) From the options below the Input heading, you're able to adjust the sensitivity of the controller, which has a direct impact on your control over your soldier, as well as your aiming accuracy when playing Fortnite: Battle Royale.

Game

Invert Aircraft Keyboard Controls	◄ On ►	
Invert Aircraft Mouse Controls	◄ Off ►	
Mouse Sensitivity Multiplier For A	2	

Camera and Display

Anonymous Mode	◄ Off ►	
Hide Other Player Names	◄ On ►	
Hidden Matchmaking Delay	0	
HUD Scale	0.85	
Show Spectator Count	◄ On ►	
Peripheral Lighting	◄ On ►	

Pings, Markers and Indicators

Mark Danger When Targeting	◄ On ►	

Control Options

Toggle Sprint	◄ Off ►	
Sprint by Default	◄ Off ►	

5:32 PM goldengamer15-id
Duos

R Reset   ESC Back

Scroll down on the Game submenu (shown here on a PC), to adjust options listed below the Control Options heading and customize how certain aspects of the game react to your commands. For example, to make aiming easier, turn on the Aim Assist option. To make building more efficient, turn on the Turbo Building and Auto Material Change feature. To reduce the amount of time it takes to open doors within the game, turn on the Auto Open Doors feature, and to automatically pick up weapons and items as you find them, turn on the Auto Pickup Weapons option.

Audio		

Volumes

Music Volume	0.00
SoundFX Volume	1.00
Voice Chat Volume	0.25
Cinematics Volume	0.34

Toggles

Subtitles	◄	Off	►
Quality	◄	High	►
Voice Chat	◄	Off	►
Push To Talk	◄	Off	►
Voice Chat Input Device	◄	Default Input	►
Voice Chat Output Device	◄	Default Output	►
Allow Background Audio	◄	Off	►
Automatically Join Game Channel	◄	On	►

5:32 PM goldengamer15-id
Duos

R Reset   ESC Back

Because sound effects play an extremely important role in Fortnite: Battle Royale, *from the game's Audio submenu (shown here on a PC), you'll definitely want to consider turning down the Music Volume option. Some gamers opt to turn off the music altogether. Next, turn up the SoundFX Volume. You want to hear all of the game's sound effects clearly. If you'll be using the game's Voice Chat mode to communicate with your partner or squad mates, also turn up the Voice Chat Volume option.*

Don't Focus Too Much on the Game Settings Used by Top-Ranked Players

Many of the top-ranked *Fortnite: Battle Royale* gamers publish details about exactly what game equipment they use, as well as the customizations they've made to the various Settings menu and submenu options. While this information is useful for reference, for several reasons, you should not try to replicate another gamer's exact settings.

First, unless you have exactly the same gaming equipment and Internet connection speed used by the pro gamer, when you replicate their settings, you'll achieve different results on your own gaming system.

Second, every pro gamer tweaks the game based on their unique gaming style and experience level. If you play using a different style, or your reflexes and game-related muscle memory are not as developed as the pro gamer, copying their game Settings will actually be detrimental to your success.

As a newb, you're better off leaving the majority of the *Fortnite: Battle Royale* Settings menu options at their Default settings. Then, once you start getting good at playing, tweak the options you believe will improve your game play. Always make small, incremental adjustments to one setting at a time, and then test out how each change works for you by playing one or two matches. Continue to tweak the settings as you deem necessary.

To discover the gaming equipment and customized settings used by top-ranked and pro *Fortnite: Battle Royale* gamers, check out these websites:

- **Best Fortnite Settings—**https://bestfortnitesettings.com/best-fortnite-pro-settings
- **Fortnite Base—**https://fortbase.net/pro-players

- **Fortnite Pro Settings & Config—**https://fortniteconfig.com
- **GamingScan—**www.gamingscan.com/fortnite-competitive-settings-gear
- **ProNettings.net—**https://prosettings.net/best-fortnite-settings-list

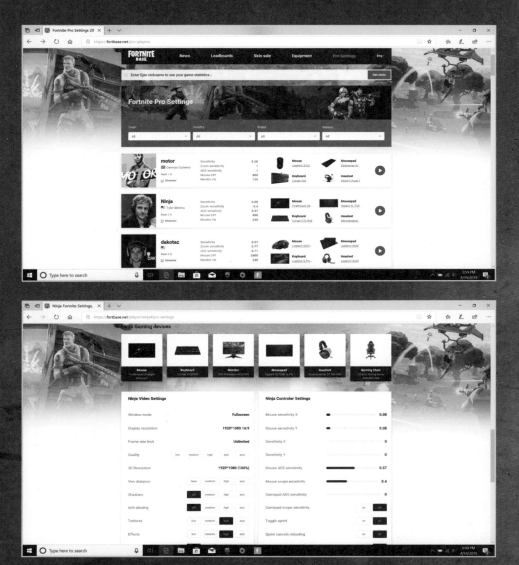

From the independent Fortnite Base website (https://fortbase.net/pro-players), for example, you can look up the player stats, ranking, gaming equipment list, and game-related settings for many of the best Fortnite: Battle Royale *players in the world. Shown here is the information from Ninja.*

How to Make In-Game Purchases

While you can play *Fortnite: Battle Royale* as much as you'd like on your favorite gaming systems for free, if you want to participate in Battle Pass Challenges or purchase items that allow you to customize the appearance of your soldier, for example, you'll need to spend real money.

To make in-game purchases, first visit the Store by selecting the Store tab that's displayed at the top of the Lobby screen.

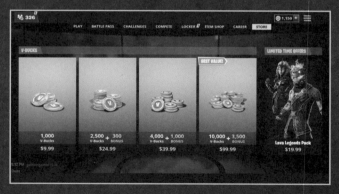

From the Store, acquire V-Bucks. This is Fortnite: Battle Royale's *in-game currency. You can purchase bundles of V-Bucks using real money. The larger the bundle of V-Bucks you purchase at once, the more money you'll save. As you can see here, 1,000 V-Bucks costs $9.99 (US), 2,800 V-Bucks costs $24.99 (US), 5,000 V-Bucks costs $39.99 (US), and 13,500 V-Bucks costs $99.99 (US).*

In conjunction with each new gaming season, Epic Games offers at least one special V-Bucks Bundle. This typically includes 600 V-Bucks plus an exclusive outfit that's only available for a limited time.

At the start of Season 8, for example, this Cobalt outfit with matching Back Bling was made available as part of the Cobalt Pack for a discounted price of $4.99 (US). This outfit will never be sold in the Item Shop, and after Season 8 ended, it probably won't ever become available again.

As soon as you purchase the Cobalt Pack, or whatever limited-time pack is available during the current season, the outfit and related accessories will immediately be added to your Locker.

Toward the end of Season 8, this Lava Legends Pack was offered for $19.99 (US). It included two outfits, along with a special Glider design, and two Back Bling designs.

Customize the Appearance of Your Soldier

Prior to each match, you have the ability to customize the appearance of your soldier in several ways, using items you've purchased or unlocked, and that are available from the Locker.

Some available outfits are larger than others, however, *Fortnite: Battle Royale* has balanced the "hit box" associated with each outfit to make them all exactly the same. In other words, whether or not an enemy is difficult to target and hit with a weapon depends almost entirely on the gamer controlling that soldier, regardless of the physical size or appearance of a soldier's outfit.

After selecting the Outfit slot from the Locker screen, this Select Outfit screen is displayed. Choose which outfit you want your soldier to wear during the upcoming match. Your selection will remain saved for all future matches, until you return to this menu and select a different outfit.

From the Lobby, select the Locker tab that's displayed at the top of the screen. On the left side of the screen are a selection of slots. Each slot represents a different customization option. On the right side of the screen is your soldier's current appearance, based on the currently selected options.

Near the top-left corner of the Locker screen is the Outfit slot. (It currently has a yellow frame around it.) Select this to choose from any of the outfits that you've previously purchased or unlocked.

Directly below the Outfit heading, near the top-center of the screen, are five icons used to sort your Outfit inventory. Options include: All (view all of your available outfits), New (display only your newest outfits), Favorite (display the outfits you've labeled as Favorites), Styles (display outfits that have optional Styles that can be unlocked to alter their appearance), Reactive (view outfits that are classified as Reactive). A Reactive outfit changes based on the way you play, or what happens to your soldier during a match.

Choose your desired outfit and click on the Save and Exit button to return to the main Locker screen.

When choosing an outfit, keep in mind that bright colors attract attention and can make your soldier easier to spot on the island, especially when exploring snow or ice-covered terrain. In lush tropical areas, camouflage colors will help your soldier blend in more. While in desert areas, outfits with tan, black, or brown-related colors might work best if your goal is to avoid being noticed.

To the right of the Outfit slot on the Locker screen is the Back Bling slot. Click on this to choose a Back Bling (backpack) design to go with the outfit you've selected. Some outfits come with a matching Back Bling design. You're always free to choose any available Back Bling design to go with any outfit from the Locker. Like everything else available from the Locker, the Back Bling you add is for cosmetic purposes only.

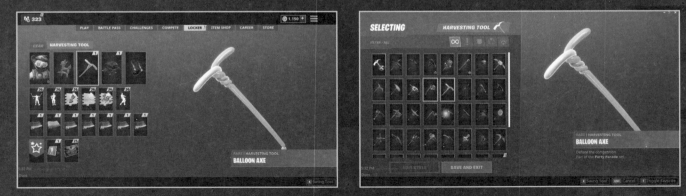

Back at the Locker screen, to the right of the Back Bling slot, is the Harvesting Tool slot. It currently has a yellow frame around it. Select it, and then choose from the available Harvesting Tool designs that you've purchased or unlocked, and that are available to your soldier. While the appearance of the different Harvesting Tools varies greatly, they all function exactly the same way during matches.

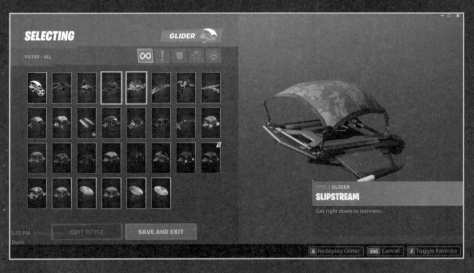

To the right of the Harvesting Tool slot on the Locker screen is the Glider slot. Select it, and then choose from the available Glider designs that you've purchased or previously unlocked, and that are currently available to your soldier. Once again, the appearances of the Glider designs vary greatly, but they all function exactly the same way.

Your soldier's Glider is used to reduce their rate of descent at the start of the match, to stop their freefall from the Battle Bus, and ensure a safe landing on the island.

The Glider can also be used at certain times during a match to transport your soldier from one location to another. To accomplish this, you'll first need to find and grab a Glider item, for example, and add it to your soldier's inventory. Then, when your soldier leaps off of a mountain, building, structure, or cliff, select and activate the Glider item to deploy the Glider and keep your soldier from falling to the ground and getting injured (or worse). Perfect timing is essential when using this item.

Displayed to the right of the Glider slot on the Locker screen is the Contrail slot. Select this, and then choose a Contrail design that you've previously unlocked. This is an animation that's displayed from your soldier's hands and/or feet during their freefall from the Battle Bus. Again, it's for cosmetic purposes only.

Displaying a Contrail during your soldier's free fall to the island does *not* speed up your soldier's descent or give you added navigational control. Contrail designs must be unlocked within the game by completing various (free) challenges or Battle Pass Challenges. They typically cannot be purchased from the Item Shop.

The second row of slots displayed on the Locker screen are used to select six different emotes that your soldier can showcase in the pre-deployment area or anytime during a match.

There are several types of emotes available, including Dance Moves, Emoticons, Spray Paint Tags, and Toys. Place a different Emote within each of the six slots.

While in the pre-deployment area or during a match, access this Emotes menu to select and showcase an emote. If you're using a keyboard/mouse combo, press the key or mouse button you have assigned to a specific Emote slots to showcase that emote, or access the Emotes menu. There are hundreds of Emotes (including many different Dance Moves) to choose from. Some can be purchased from the Item Shop, while others need to be unlocked by completing challenges.

Emoticons are graphic icons that your soldier can toss into the air for everyone in the nearby area to see.

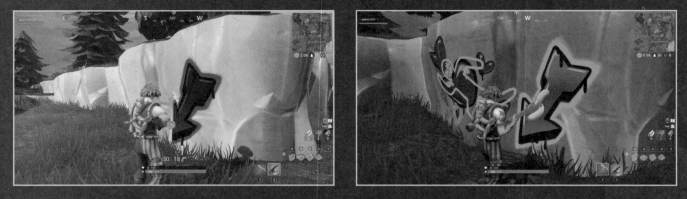

Spray Paint Tags allow you to spray paint any flat object on the island, such as the wall of a building or structure. You're able to mix and match Spray Paint Tags to create original graffiti designs and leave your mark.

Emotes can be used to communicate with your partner or squad members, to taunt enemies, to showcase your soldier's personality, or just to have fun while exploring the island as you participate in matches. As you'll discover, there are hundreds of different Emotes to unlock, purchase, and then choose from, but you can only have access to six per match, so choose wisely.

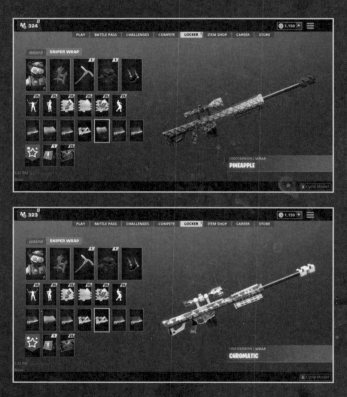

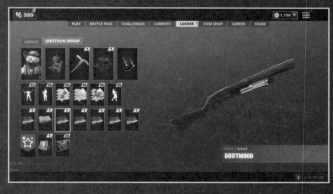

The third row of slots displayed on the Locker Screen allow you to customize the appearance of vehicles and weapons using wraps that you've unlocked. First click on one of the six Wraps slots, and then select one of the customizable Wrap options that are currently available to you. (Wraps do not alter the functionality of a weapon or vehicle, only their appearance.)

Above is a Sniper Rifle with the Pineapple Wrap. Below is the same weapon with a Chromatic Wrap.

The fourth row of slots on the Locker screen allow you to choose a custom Banner, select which background music track you want to hear, and choose your Loading Screen (seen each time you launch Fortnite: Battle Royale). One at a time, click on a slot and then choose from the available options. Shown here, the Loading Screen slot was chosen, and one of the available graphic options is being selected. Like everything else in the Locker, this has no impact on actual game play.

Visit the Item Shop

Every day within the Item Shop, a different selection of outfits, Back Bling designs, Harvesting Tool designs, Glider designs, and Emotes are made available for sale. All of these items are optional and can be purchased using V-Bucks. After visiting the Store to acquire a bundle of V-Bucks, from the Lobby, access the Item Shop to purchase items one at a time.

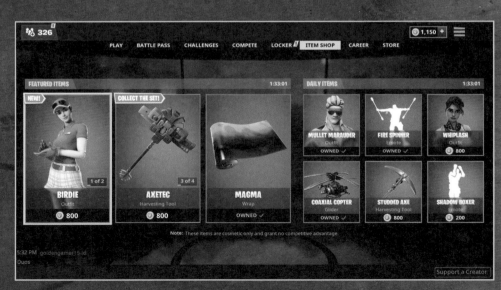

On the left side of the Item Shop, below the Featured Items heading, will be at least two different items per day. These slots tend to showcase the newest, rarest, or most exclusive outfits or items currently available.

When you see a showcased item you want, highlight and select it. The Purchase screen for that item gets displayed. Choose the Purchase Item(s) button to confirm the purchase. As soon as you do this, the selected item (or items if it's an outfit and Back Bling design bundle, for example) become available immediately within the Locker.

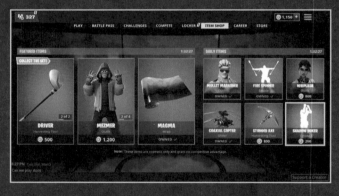

On the right side of the Item Shop are typically six additional items, all displayed below the Daily Items heading. These tend to be items that are more common, and that get re-introduced into the game periodically. This is also where you'll find Dance Move emotes (each sold separately). Be sure to check the Item Shop each day to see the latest selection of items being offered.

Outfits that are categorized as Legendary are the most exclusive. These are rarely, if ever, re-introduced into the game, and they're only made available for a limited time. These also tend to be the most expensive. Most Legendary outfits come with a matching Back Bling design. While a Rare outfit will typically cost 1,200 V-Bucks (about $12.00 US), a Legendary

outfit typically costs 2,000 V-Bucks, which translates to approximately $20.00 (US).

Shown here is the Whiplash outfit. It's priced at 800 V-Bucks (approximately $8.00 US). This outfit is part of the Racer Royale set and is classified as Uncommon. When an outfit is part of a set, this means that other matching items, such as a Back Bling design, Harvesting Tool design, and/or Glider design have also been released. As you can see here, the outfit's matching Back Bling design is included, but other matching items in the set are sold separately.

Mezmer is an example of a Rare outfit. These tend to be priced at 1,200 V-Bucks (approximately $12.00 US). As you can see, this one is part of the Sun Soldiers set. It comes with matching Back Bling.

Depending on the outfit you choose, you're able to make your soldier look intimidating, whimsical, or menacing, for example. There are also plenty of outfits that are released in conjunction with storylines happening within the current gaming season, or that relate to a

Whichever outfit you choose, remember that it offers no competitive advantage whatsoever during a match, yet by mixing and matching different outfits with accessory items (like Back Bling and a Harvesting Tool), you can make your soldier look truly unique within the game. All items you purchase or unlock are yours to keep forever and get stored within the Locker that's linked with your Epic Games account.

Purchase a Current Battle Pass

Every gaming season, Epic Games releases a new Fortnite: Battle Royale *Battle Pass (each sold separately). A Battle Pass allows gamers to participate in Tier-based challenges. A typical Battle Pass includes 100 Tiers. Each time you complete a challenge, it unlocks a prize, such as an outfit, Back Bling design, Harvesting Tool design, Glider design, Contrail design, some type of Emote, a Loading Screen graphic, a bundle of 100 V-Bucks, or another item.*

Each Battle Pass includes several outfits that are exclusive. This means they probably won't ever be released elsewhere, such as from the Item Shop. Each gaming season lasts for approximately three months, after which time the Battle Pass expires and a new one is introduced. All of the prizes that you unlock by completing or unlocking Tier challenges are yours to keep forever.

At the time you purchase a new Battle Pass, consider upgrading your purchase to a Battle Bundle. This typically costs 2,800 V-Bucks (approximately $28.00 US). Upon purchasing a Battle Bundle, you'll automatically unlock the first 25 Battle Pass Tiers and receive those prizes instantly.

In addition to purchasing a Battle Pass, which costs 950 V-Bucks (approximately $9.50 US), if you don't want to complete any of the separate Tier-based challenges, you can pay a flat fee of 150 V-Bucks (about $1.50 US) to unlock individual Tiers. To obtain all of the perks possible from all of a season's Battle Pass Tiers, you must complete or purchase them during that gaming season.

To purchase a Battle Pass, see the Tier-related prizes associated with the Battle Pass, or to unlock individual Tiers, from the Lobby, select the Battle Pass option at the top of the screen. Shown here is the Battle Pass screen for Season 8. Three Tiers are about to be purchased at once for 450 V-Bucks.

Once you've selected your gaming hardware, tweaked various game options from Fortnite: Battle Royale's Settings menu, and you've visited the Locker prior to a match to customize the appearance of your soldier, return to the Lobby screen. You're now ready to experience a match!

In addition to the Battle Pass Tier-related challenges, by selecting the Challenges tab from the Lobby, you're able to participate in additional Daily and Weekly challenges, as well as Event challenges and Style challenges. Completing any of these challenges also allows you to win prizes.

SECTION 2

WELCOME TO THE MYSTERIOUS ISLAND

Regardless of which *Fortnite: Battle Royale* game play mode you choose to experience, every match takes place on the mysterious island. During any gaming season, the island will be comprised of approximately 20 labeled points of interest, along with many unlabeled areas for you to explore and within which you'll likely encounter enemies to battle and hopefully defeat.

When looking at the Island Map, along the top of the screen are the letters "A" through "J." Going down the left side of the map are the numbers "1" through "10." To help you navigate your way around the island, each labeled point of interest can be found at specific coordinates. For example, midway through Season 8, Sunny Steps could be found at coordinates I2.5, and Tilted Towers could be found at coordinates D5.5.

As you're viewing the Island Map, it's possible to zoom in on specific areas so you can see greater detail. Shown here is the Pleasant Park region of the island, found at map coordinates C3.5.

This area of the island, called Paradise Palms (map coordinates I8), is a small urban area that during this gaming season was surrounded by desert terrain.

Use Markers to Help You Navigate Around the Island

It's also from the Island Map that you're able to place a Marker. This can be done while in the pre-deployment area or while aboard the Battle Bus to pinpoint your desired landing destination, or at any time during a match to make it easier to navigate toward a specific location on the island. Shown here, a blue Marker has been placed on the Season 8 Island Map, in the center of Prudiz's Block (near map coordinates D2).

As you can see here, when viewing the main game screen, a Marker looks like a colored flare that can be seen from a distance. The Marker was placed while the soldier was in the pre-deployment area, so it can clearly be seen from far away during his freefall and subsequent Glider landing on the island.

The same blue Marker is seen here, as the soldier approaches Prudiz's Block on foot after landing on the island.

Markers are especially useful when playing with a partner or squad mates, because they can be used to set a rendezvous location. Each gamer is assigned a different Marker color. As you can see here; during this Squads match, all four gamers have set a Marker near the same landing location (in Pleasant Park) and plan to meet up as soon as their soldiers land on the island.

Keep in mind, only you, your partner, or your squad mates can see each other's Markers. Your enemies can't see them, nor can you see Markers placed by your adversaries.

Choose Your Landing Location at the Start of the Match

While in the pre-deployment area, and while the Battle Bus is traveling across the island, the random route the bus will travel at the start of the current match is temporarily displayed using a line that's comprised of arrow-shaped icons. The direction the arrows are facing is the direction the Battle Bus is traveling.

Once you know the random path the Battle Bus will take at the start of a match, you're in a better position to choose your soldier's desired landing spot on the island. What you'll discover is that any point of interest that's close to the beginning or very end of the Battle Bus's route will always be popular, so you're virtually guaranteed to encounter enemies almost immediately upon landing.

Points of interest located near the center of the island (such as Neo Towers) also tend to be extremely popular, because your soldier likely won't need to travel great distances to avoid the storm once it forms.

During the current gaming season, whatever the newly added labeled points of interest are on the island will also be popular, meaning that you'll likely encounter a lot of enemies immediately upon landing. (Because it was new, Sunny Steps was a popular point of interest during Season 8 and Season 9.)

Upon landing on the island at the start of a match, your soldier will only be equipped with their Harvesting Tool. This can be used as a weapon, but it'll take several close-range strikes on an enemy to do any serious damage. The Harvesting Tool (your soldier's pickaxe) is no match against an enemy soldier armed with any type of gun or weapon.

If you choose a popular landing spot at the start of a match and you're not the first soldier to reach that location, chances are you'll discover multiple enemies who beat you there will already have grabbed a weapon and will be waiting for you to land, so they can attack while you're still unarmed. So, if you notice other soldiers landing before you during the final moments of your soldier's descent from the Battle Bus, use the navigational controls to quickly choose an alternate landing spot or you'll likely wind up being eliminated within seconds after landing.

This soldier landed on a building rooftop in what was formerly called Tilted Towers (a popular point of interest), but didn't have time to grab a nearby weapon before being shot and defeated within seconds of his arrival.

Anytime you opt to land in a popular area on the map, your first objective is to quickly grab a weapon (any weapon) and ammo, so you can defend yourself, and attack any enemies that land in close proximity after your soldier. During the final moments of your descent, you should be able to see the glow of chests or the reflection of weapons that are lying out in the open, either on the ground, or on the top of a building or structure, for example.

Especially if you're a newb, it's a smart strategy to choose a landing location that is not directly within a popular point of interest. This reduces your chances of encountering enemies right away and gives you more time to gather an arsenal and prepare for firefights.

Located just outside almost every labeled point of interest on the map, you'll find one or more small structures. Either on, near, or within these structures, you're apt to find weapons, ammo, and useful loot items. If you're lucky, you'll also discover a nearby chest or Loot Llama, for example, or perhaps a vehicle that'll allow you to travel around the island faster.

If you want extra time to build up your soldier's arsenal and be able to explore the island a bit before encountering enemies, consider landing at a remote location on the map. In this case, the soldier landed in the outskirts of Lonely Lodge, on top of a tall wooden tower (near map coordinates J5.5).

There are many remote locations that are not close to a major point of interest. You'll typically find these around the outskirts of the island, although some are inland and also offer plenty of loot and weapons to collect.

Within minutes of landing on the island, in addition to having to contend with enemy soldiers, a deadly storm will form, and then periodically expand and move around the island, making more and more of the terrain uninhabitable. Shown here, a soldier is caught in the storm and is running as fast as possible to the safe area of the island.

Beware of the Deadly Storm!

For every second your soldier is caught within the deadly storm (on the wrong side of the blue wall and outside of the circle depicted on the Island Map), some of their Health will be depleted. If you look at this soldier's Health meter, he's only sustained 12 points worth of damage thus far. Your soldier's shields do not protect them from the deadly impact of the storm. If too much time is spent within the storm, your soldier will eventually perish.

During the early stages of a match, the amount of damage your soldier receives during each second they're caught within the storm will be minimal. However, the speed at which their Health meter gets depleted while caught in the storm will increase as the match progresses.

Located just below the mini-map that's displayed on the main game screen is a timer that'll tell you when the storm will next be expanding and moving. You'll also see warning messages appear periodically in the center of the screen. This soldier has only 34 seconds remaining before the storm expands and moves again. Based on the white line that's displayed within the mini-map, it's obvious that the solider will need to hustle in order to get back into the safe zone once the storm expands.

To see the current safe area of the island and determine where the storm will be expanding and moving to next, refer to the Island Map during a match. When one circle appears on the Island Map, it's within this area that's the safe terrain. Any area that's displayed in pink has become uninhabitable as a result of the storm and should be avoided. In this case, the storm has not yet reached the island, but in just 16 seconds it'll start forming. You can see the soldier's location (near map coordinates F9.5) is far away from the circle (where the storm will be moving).

When two circles are displayed on the Island Map, the outer circle shows you the area that's currently safe on the island. The inner circle shows you where the storm will be moving to next and where the safe area of the island will be. The white line displayed on both the Island Map and the mini-map shows you the fastest and most direct route to follow in order to avoid the storm. The pink area is uninhabitable and has already been ravaged by the storm.

Especially if your soldier needs to travel a far distance in order to avoid the storm, this can seldom be done simply by walking or even running. In other words, you'll need to utilize a vehicle or another transportation option (such as a Rift-To-Go, Launch Pad, Zipline, or a Slipstream) to help your soldier travel faster. Based on where you are on the island, having a good knowledge of the terrain will often help you quickly find a vehicle or transportation option.

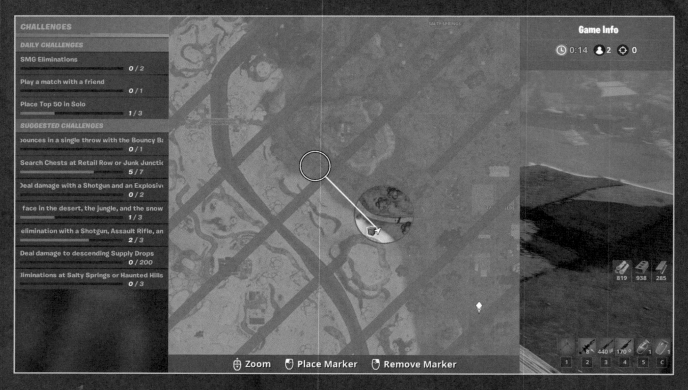

If you make it into the End Game (the final few minutes of a match), the inhabitable area will become very small. Instead of getting even smaller every few minutes, the location of the safe circle will move from one location to another on the map. (The zoom feature of the Island Map is used here.) An additional challenge becomes staying within the safe area as this tiny circle of safe space moves around. At the same time, you'll be dealing with the remaining enemies still in the match who are looking to annihilate you.

Use Vehicles and Transportation Options to Help You Travel Around Faster

During every gaming season, there are a variety of transportation options available to you that'll make it faster to travel around the island, outrun the storm, avoid enemy attacks, launch your own attacks, and explore more efficiently. Your soldier also has the ability to walk, run, crouch, and tiptoe around the island. However, even when running, this is seldom the fastest way to get around.

Aside from moving around on foot, there are three other types of transportation available during each match. Even if some of these transportation methods have been vaulted for Solo, Duos, and Squads matches, they're typically still available within the Creative game play mode, and sometimes become available in temporary game play modes released by Epic Games.

Natural Island Phenomenon

Depending on the gaming season, non-vehicle transportation options might include Rifts, Ziplines, Geysers, and/or ice-covered lakes (that cause your soldier's feet to freeze into ice cubes, so he can glide across mainly flat surfaces at a fast speed).

These transportation options are typically randomly found on the island. When your soldier steps into a Rift or Geyser, for example, he'll be catapulted high into the air. Use your navigational controls to help guide your soldier while they are airborne, to reach another destination quickly.

Upon stepping onto a Geyser, your soldier will fly high up into the air. As they make their way back toward land, their Glider will automatically deploy to ensure a safe landing.

A soldier can step into a Rift that occurs randomly on the island, typically in desert areas. Rifts can only be used when and where they are found. They cannot be moved, collected, or stored. After being launched into the air, as they make their way back toward land, your soldier's Glider will automatically deploy to ensure a safe landing. This is different from a Rift-To-Go item, which can be collected, stored, and then used anytime it's convenient. (A Rift-To-Go item, however, takes up one of your soldier's six inventory slots.)

Transportation-Related Items

The selection of these transportation-related items constantly changes with each gaming season. These are items that can be found, collected, stored within your soldier's inventory, and then used when needed. Examples of transportation-related items include: Launch Pads, Grapplers, Balloons, Glider items, and Rift-To-Go items.

Which items you should use to get around will depend several factors, including:

- Which item(s) you have in your soldier's inventory.
- The type of terrain your soldier is in and how far they need to travel.
- Since some travel-related items (such as a Grappler) require perfect timing and accurate aim to use effectively, how much practice you've had using the item will determine how useful it is to your solider.
- Whether or not you have time to set up an item, such as a Launch Pad, and then use it, or if you need something that works instantly so you can begin traveling faster or get away from your soldier's current location immediately.

- The speed you want to travel. While Balloons allow you to travel great distances, the speed you'll travel is much slower than using a Launch Pad, Grappler, Glider item, or most vehicles, for example.

- Some items are ideal for traveling up and down—such as to go from ground level to the top of a nearby building or structure—while others are better suited for covering horizontal distances. Some items are better suited for any travel needs. For example, a Glider item can be used for going from the top of a tall building, structure, or mountain to the bottom of it, but it's not useful for going upward.

- Whether or not you want to make it easier for other soldiers (friends or foes) to follow you. A Launch Pad can be used repeatedly by any number of soldiers. Another soldier can follow you into a Rift (or Rift-To-Go), but only for a few seconds after you travel through it. Other items (like Balloons or a Grappler) can only be used by your soldier. Another soldier can follow your movements only if they have that same item in their inventory and choose to use it at the same time as you.

A Launch Pad, Grappler (shown on the left), Glider item (shown on the right), Balloons, or Rift-To-Go, for example, might be found lying on the ground, out in the open. They're also sometimes found within chests, Loot Llamas, Vending Machines, and/or within Supply Drops. Each is used in a slightly different way, but all can be used to travel across a lot of territory quickly.

Upon adding Balloons to your soldier's inventory, you can activate one, two, or three of them (out of 10) at a time. Balloons were vaulted from Solo, Duos, and Squads modes at the start of Season 9, but could be returned to the game at anytime. Balloons continue to be available in some other game play modes.

One Balloon will allow your soldier to jump higher and leap farther (compared to when not using any item). Using Balloons are not the fastest possible mode of transportation, but they make no noise. Their biggest drawback is that the Balloons are bright and colorful, so they're easy for enemies to spot (and potentially shoot down) from a distance. If your soldier is floating up high and their Balloons get shot at and destroyed, they'll crash back to land and likely perish. While it makes the soldier more of a visible target, one Balloon can potentially be worn for extended periods of time as the soldier wanders around the island.

Using three Balloons at once, your soldier will automatically soar into the air and keep going up until they reach a maximum height, at which point one Balloon will automatically pop and they'll slowly descend back toward land. Use the directional controls to navigate.

Two Balloons increase the height and distance a soldier can achieve when jumping. They'll remain airborne longer, and you'll have some navigational control while your soldier is in mid-air or landing. Keep in mind, if you pop both Balloons too soon (or the Balloons get shot at and popped by an enemy) and your soldier falls too far before landing, he'll perish.

Here's what a Launch Pad looks like once it's been set up on a flat surface. On the plus side, you can use a Launch Pad as often as you'd like. The drawback is that it takes a few seconds to set up and it must be placed on a flat surface. A Launch Pad does not require an inventory slot for your soldier to carry it. This item gets stored in your soldier's inventory with their resources. Once it's been set up, it can't be moved.

When building a fortress, especially during the End Game (the final minutes of a match), place a Launch Pad on the roof of the fortress or on a platform near the top of it, so your soldier can make a quick escape and relocate to another area within the final circle.

A Glider item can be picked up, carried, and then launched up to 10 times. To activate it, your soldier must leap off the top of a high surface, such as a cliff, ramp, or building. Perfect timing is essential to activate the Glider, or your soldier will simply fall to the ground and potentially perish. During this End Game portion of a match, this soldier has just defeated an enemy, is drinking a Small Shield Potion to replenish her shields, and can then grab the Glider item that was left behind by a defeated soldier.

Using a Grappler, your soldier can aim at the top of a tall tree, building, or structure, for example. When the grappling hook reaches its target, your soldier will be quickly pulled toward the target location. This tool can be used to quickly reach the top of a building or structure. If you use it with perfect timing, it can also allow your soldier to swing from target to target, like Spider-Man®.

In addition to a handheld Grappler item, there's a Grappler built into the Baller vehicle, which can be used to latch onto an object and then swing the Baller (with a soldier inside) from target to target.

At least through Season 8 (possibly longer), a growing portion of the island contained a network of pre-created ziplines that could be ridden by soldiers to quickly travel from one point to another.

At any point while riding a zipline, your soldier can leap from their airborne ride and fall to the ground. If they're high up, however, this will result in injury, or possibly cause them to perish as a result of the fall.

Multiple soldiers can ride the same zipline at once. If two soldiers are travelling in opposite directions and wind up crashing, both will immediately fall to the ground. If it's a long way down, they're both likely to perish. It's better to quickly switch traveling directions to avoid a crash.

Hop into the Driver's Seat of a Vehicle

There are a variety of vehicle types that are either randomly placed throughout the island, or that can be found within certain types of terrain or areas.

Examples of vehicles that you may encounter (although the selection changes from gaming season to gaming season) include: ATKs (All-Terrain Karts), Quadcrashers, Hoverboards (also called Drift Boards), Ballers, Cannons, Shopping Carts, and X-4 Stormwing airplanes.

While riding a zipline, a soldier can aim and shoot their active weapon. It's also possible to turn around and switch traveling directions while riding a zipline, or to stop altogether at any point along the zipline's path. Stopping makes it easier to accurately target a weapon at an enemy below.

An ATK is a souped-up golf cart. It can be driven around on any terrain type, but it makes a lot of noise, so your enemies will hear its approach. It also takes damage rather easily. Once the ATK's HP meter hits zero the vehicle automatically gets destroyed and disappears.

Once inside a Baller, your soldier can roll and bounce around the island. It can crash into almost anything. To speed up, use the Boost feature. Using the built-in grappling hook, a Baller can reach high-up objects or structures, or slingshot between items. While riding within a Baller, your soldier can go airborne and take zero damage upon landing. This vehicle makes little noise, but while driving a Baller, a soldier cannot use any weapons or build anything.

A Quadcrasher is fast. This type of vehicle allows your soldier to cross any type of terrain. This vehicle makes noise, but it can crash through barriers and go airborne. It's harder to damage than an ATK, and it also holds up to four soldiers. A Quadcrasher has a quickly recharging Boost feature that allows its travel speed to increase for a few seconds at a time.

Ballers are very maneuverable and can go airborne, but they can be shot at and destroyed by enemy attacks.

The driver of an ATK, Quadcrasher, or Baller cannot use a weapon or item while driving. If the vehicle holds one or more passengers, however, the passengers can use their weapon or items while in the moving vehicle. Shown here is a Quadcrasher with its Boost feature activated. This allows the vehicle to shoot forward and travel at a faster speed for a few seconds at a time.

Shown here is a Quadcrasher with a driver and one passenger (who is able to use their weapon or build while the vehicle is in motion).

While a Hoverboard can only transport one soldier, these are typically the fastest and most maneuverable vehicles on the island. Use it to surf over any type of terrain, go airborne, and cover a lot of territory quickly. One benefit to riding on a Hoverboard is that your soldier can simultaneously shoot their weapon or use other offensive or defensive items.

X-4 Stormwing airplanes were only featured within the main *Fortnite: Battle Royale* game play modes for a short time before being vaulted. While they could make a return in the future when playing Solo, Duos, or Squads matches, these airplanes sometimes appear within temporary game play modes offered by Epic Games and can be added to games created using the Creative game play mode.

At the start of Season 9, a network of Slipstreams were introduced onto the island. These too can be used to help your soldier get around parts of the island faster than on foot.

SECTION 3

GET TO KNOW THE TERRAIN

The mysterious island always offers many exciting and sometimes dangerous places to visit. Based on the random travel route the Battle Bus follows, as well as the expansion and movement of the storm, and the actions of your enemies, where you'll wind up visiting during each match will vary greatly from match to match.

The Island Is Constantly Evolving

As you know, from season to season, the island map transforms a lot. While you want to become familiar with the labeled points of interest (locations) on the map during each gaming season, what's equally important is understanding the many different types of terrain and climates you'll discover.

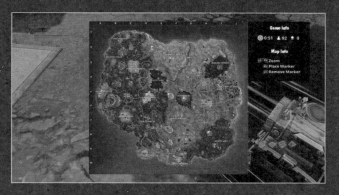

This is what the Island Map looked like during Season 4. It featured several labeled points of interest, such as Risky Reels, Anarchy Acres, and Moisty Mire, that no longer exist on the island.

Toward the end of Season 8, this is how the island looked. As you can see, during that gaming season, some of the island was covered with snow and ice, and there was a volcanic area (featuring hot lava flows) surrounding a massive volcano as well.

This is how the island looked at the start of Season 9. You'll notice a few new labeled points of interest, along with additional places to explore that are not labeled on the map. Plus, several popular locations, such as Tilted Towers (now called Neo Tilted) were revamped.

Always Use the Terrain You're in to Your Advantage

Using the terrain around you at any given moment can help you stay alive longer. When necessary, use the terrain to help you launch more effective attacks against your enemies. For example, climb up to the top of a hill, mountain, or tall building, and then shoot at enemies lurking below.

Connecting many labeled points of interest on the island are a network of paved roads and dirt paths. These can help you get to where you're going faster, but following roads or paths is not always the safest route to take.

In some cases, what separates specific points of interest is a vast open space or a series of hills and mountains.

Anytime you're traveling between labeled points of interest on the map, it's important to keep moving, and avoid open spaces whenever possible. When your soldier is traveling through an open space, along a road, or across an open area, they can easily be seen (and often heard) by enemies and easily attacked. Savvy gamers find a hiding spot along (or above) a road or open space and then wait for newbs to pass through. An enemy using a weapon with a scope attached can target a spot where they know an enemy soldier will pass through, and then start shooting as soon as that soldier is within their sights.

If you're forced to travel across a vast open space (or follow a road or path), keep moving in a zigzag and unpredictable pattern, and randomly jump into the air. Make your soldier a fast-moving target that's difficult to shoot at.

When driving any type of vehicle (such as a Baller), also follow a random route that involves lots of sharp and unexpected turns. If the vehicle has a Turbo or Boost feature, use it periodically to alter the vehicle's speed.

As you're traveling along roads, paths, or across open areas, remember that enemy attacks can originate from any direction, including from above.

If there are no objects already on the island, such as rock formations, trees, or broken-down vehicles to hide behind and use as shielding, be prepared to have your soldier enter into building mode and construct their own barrier or fortress using wood, stone, or metal tiles.

To build a quick barrier to use as shielding that works almost anywhere, first build a vertical wall made of stone or metal, and then immediately behind it, build a ramp/staircase. When your soldier crouches down and hides behind this simple structure, an enemy will need to shoot through two layers of tiles before hitting your soldier.

Consider adding walls to either side of the structure to protect your soldier from flank attacks (from the side).

Almost anywhere on the island, if you need to quickly obtain a height advantage over your enemies, build a ramp. Wood is the quickest material to build with, but it's also the easiest to destroy.

Anytime you build a small fortress with four walls around your soldier for protection, don't forget to add a roof. It's easy for an enemy to get up higher than your fortress and then shoot down into where your soldier is hiding, or simply drop a few explosive weapons into your fortress.

As you're building and climbing a ramp, if your soldier is up high and an enemy manages to shoot and destroy just one tile near the bottom of the ramp, the entire ramp will come crashing down and be destroyed. Your soldier will likely fall to the ground and be eliminated from the match. If you notice an enemy soldier on a tall ramp, instead of trying to target that moving enemy with your soldier's weapon, simply destroy a low-down ramp tile, which is a non-moving and easier-to-hit target.

The wooden ramp you see here (closest to the soldier) has been reinforced. Although it's made of wood, it'll be harder to destroy with bullets or explosives.

Most vehicles can easily travel up and down ramps that are built on the island and can also cross over bridges that are built using wood, stone, or metal tiles. Depending on the type of vehicle being used, driving through deep water will slow down the vehicle. When driving over a bridge, your soldier can travel across bodies of water much faster.

Keep in mind, the driver of a vehicle cannot build and drive at the same time. However, if your vehicle also has a passenger, your partner or squad mate can build a ramp or bridge while the other soldier drives. This is useful when playing a Duos or Squads match, for example.

Regardless of where you are on the island, weapons, ammo, loot items, and other objects can typically be found and collected once. Likewise, each chest, Loot Llama, Vending Machine, and Supply Drop can only be opened or used once per match. Thus, in addition to knowing the best places to find useful weapons, ammo, loot items, and objects, it's essential that your soldier be the first to arrive at a particular location to grab what's there.

Vending Machines are scattered randomly throughout the island. To acquire what is offered by a Vending Machine, it used to be necessary to make purchases using wood, stone, or metal. As long as you had ample resources, you could purchase as much as you wanted from each Vending Machine. This is no longer the case. Now, when a soldier approaches a Vending Machine, he can choose one item that's being offered and receive it for free. After a Vending Machine is used once, it self-destructs and disappears for the rest of the match.

If you discover a Vending Machine that offers a selection of powerful weapons or loot items, but it contains nothing you need for your soldier's arsenal, consider hiding out somewhere near that Vending Machine. Using a long-distance weapon with a scope, target the Vending Machine. As soon as an enemy approaches the Vending Machine and acquires an item from it, shoot and defeat that enemy. Not only will you be able to eliminate a soldier from the match, but you'll be able to acquire all of the weapons, ammo, loot items, and resources that soldier was carrying, including the weapon or item just retrieved from the Vending Machine.

Also, instead of approaching chests, Loot Llamas, or Supply Drops, consider hiding somewhere nearby and using a long-range weapon with a scope to defeat an enemy that approaches and attempts to open one of these objects. Keep in mind that it takes several seconds to open a chest, Loot Llama, or Supply Drop, during which time that soldier is defenseless. This is the perfect time to launch an attack.

Anytime you're able to use a Sniper Rifle (or any weapon with a scope) on a non-moving target, your likelihood of hitting that target dramatically improves, especially if you've already had time to line up your shot and then can simply wait for the enemy to step into your gun's targeting crosshairs.

If you choose to approach a chest, Loot Llama, or Supply Drop, do so with extreme caution. Expect that there will be enemies lurking about waiting to attack once you approach. To protect your soldier, once you safely reach the chest, Loot Llama, or Supply Drop that's out in the open, quickly build stone or metal walls around it (don't forget to add a roof). This will provide protection while you open the object and collect what's inside. Shown here, a Loot Llama has been surrounded by a stone (brick) wall.

As you can see here, a Vending Machine has been surrounded by metal walls. This should provide enough shielding so your soldier can select and grab a weapon or item from the Vending Machine. The protective walls will then give you time to access your soldier's Inventory screen to rearrange their inventory, if needed.

When you're ready to leave the mini-fortress you've built around an object (such as a Vending Machine), simply edit one of the vertical wall tiles and add a door. Exit with the same level of caution that you used to approach the area.

The Types of Terrain You'll Typically Discover on the Island

You're about to discover strategies for exploring, fighting within, and protecting your soldier while in various types of terrain that you'll likely encounter on the island. During each match, try to remember where you discover various items, objects, and structures, for example. When you return to that spot during future matches, you'll likely discover the same (or similar) items, objects, or structures, which could be very useful.

During any particular gaming season, structures tend to stay in exactly the same place from match to match. However, items that are lying out in the open on the ground, or the location of chests, Loot Llamas, and vehicles, for example, will often be randomized.

You may find a chest in the same location during each match, but not always. If you discover a remote location upon landing on the island that offers a selection of weapons, ammo, and loot items, chances are, you'll find weapons, ammo, and loot items each time you visit that location during future matches, but the weapon, ammo, and loot item types will often vary.

Desert Terrain

What's interesting about the desert areas of the island is that there are some flat, wide-open spaces, areas that contain hills and mountains, regions where clusters of structures can be found close together, and there are areas that contain multi-level suburban structures (such as tall buildings and homes, all in close proximity).

Take Advantage of Rifts in Desert Areas

The desert region of the island where you're most apt to encounter Rifts. To use a Rift, have your soldier walk (or drive a vehicle) directly into it.

Your soldier will instantly be catapulted up into the air.

Connecting the various areas of the desert region on the island are a series of paved roads and dirt paths. Especially if you're traveling on foot, it's best to avoid following these roads and paths. Instead, cut across the desert terrain. By doing this, you're less apt to encounter enemies.

While airborne, use your directional controls to navigate toward the desired landing spot. Before crashing down on land, your soldier's Glider will deploy to ensure a safe touchdown.

Rifts occur randomly on the island. They cannot be collected or moved (like a Rift-To-Go item). Once a soldier activates a Rift, other soldiers (friends or foes) have a few seconds to follow the first soldier through before the Rift disappears.

Make Your Way Around the Desert Areas

Outside of the desert areas that contain clusters of buildings and structures, you'll discover stand-alone structures. Some are small huts, while others are multi-level buildings.

Approach each structure with caution, in case an enemy is already inside. Stand to the side of a closed door with a close- to medium-range weapon drawn and ready to fire. Before entering, listen carefully for the sound of movement inside.

Upon opening the door to a structure, peek inside and look for Traps or other potential dangers before proceeding inside and gathering whatever weapons, ammo, and loot you can find.

Notice that surrounding many of the roads are hills or mountains. If you know enemies are in the area, climb to the top of a hill or mountain while trying to remain out of sight. When you have the height advantage, wait for enemies to travel along the road below, and launch attacks whenever you have the upper hand and the element of surprise.

As always, using a gun with a scope will allow you to zoom in on a potential target and shoot with extreme accuracy from a distance (such as from the top of a mountain).

The homes you'll discover in the desert area may look a bit different than homes found in other regions of the island, but they should be explored the same way. You'll often find the best loot (including chests) in the basement or attic.

Within the various rooms of the homes, you'll often find weapons, ammo, or loot items lying on the ground, out in the open. Collect what you need and add it to your soldier's arsenal.

If the home has a garage, don't forget to search inside it. You may find a parked vehicle waiting to be commandeered, although chests and other goodies can also sometimes be found in garages that are attached to homes.

When exploring one of the more urban areas in the desert terrain, stick to the high ground as much as possible and try to launch your attacks on enemies who are below. Shown here is the tall Hotel 23 building within Paradise Palms. The soldier is standing at ground level.

Here's the view from the roof of the hotel. With the right weapon(s) in your arsenal, you can easily shoot or snipe at any targets below when your soldier has the height advantage.

To travel from one structure to another that's nearby, instead of going to ground level and walking between buildings, build a bridge that connects the two structures. This allows you to maintain a height advantage.

Just like in many more remote areas of the island, you're apt to discover abandoned trucks in the desert region. Check inside the truck, as well as on the truck's roof, for useful loot.

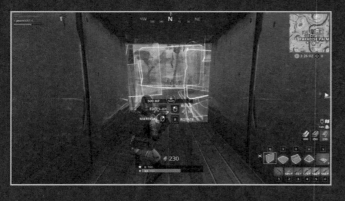

Once inside a truck, build a metal wall at the opening to protect your soldier while he's inside. Now that your soldier is protected, he has time to open the chest, rearrange his inventory, or use Health and/ or Shield power-up items. If an enemy approaches, you'll have a several second warning once you see and hear the metal wall being shot at.

The Racetrack that's located between map coordinates I6.5 and J6.5 has been a popular spot on the island for several gaming seasons. If it's still there when you experience a match, be sure to search all of the buildings that surround the track. You'll typically find lots of useful things that'll expand and improve your arsenal.

Another option while in the truck is to crouch down, aim your weapon at the door, and then wait for an enemy to approach so you can shoot him.

Located near the racetrack you'll often discover parked vehicles. If you find one, practice your driving skills by taking a few laps around the track. Keep in mind, nearby enemies will hear the engine of most vehicles and try to shoot at your vehicle as you approach. This track was originally designed to be used by ATKs, but you can test or practice your driving skills on the track using any vehicle.

Make your soldier crouch down and tiptoe through the halfway open garage door to reach the vehicle that's inside.

Anytime you're driving a Quadcrasher, notice the green circle on the right side of the vehicle. When this circle is green, the vehicle's Boost feature is available.

Activate the Boost and the vehicle will shoot forward and pick up speed for several seconds. After using Boost, it takes several seconds for the rocket engine to recharge.

A large portion of the desert terrain is found along the outer-edge of the island. As you're exploring this area, keep tabs on the location of the deadly storm, and plan for when and where it'll be moving to next. If you know you'll have to travel a far distance to escape the storm, either leave yourself plenty of time to travel on foot, or make sure you have a vehicle that'll help you escape what will soon become the storm-ravaged area quickly.

Factories and Large Structures (Including the Block)

Depending on the gaming season, large structures or factories could be part of a labeled point of interest, or they could be something you encounter as you're traveling in between popular locations on the island. The Block is also a location that's been added to the island and continues to evolve over time. It contains several large buildings and structures.

Whenever possible, try to explore a large structure starting from the rooftop and working your way down to ground level. This often gives you a tactical height advantage should you encounter enemies working their way up within the structure.

From the outside of the structure, build a ramp from the ground to get up to the roof.

Several areas of the island now have a network of Slipstreams that your soldier can travel within. Use the directional controls to navigate or switch travel directions.

Try to avoid vast open spaces within large structures. Even if you see something good in the middle of the field that's found within this indoor sporting complex, for example, reaching that item could be dangerous since you'll be out in the open. Instead, focus on areas surrounding the indoor field and look for whatever weapons, ammo, and loot items you can find.

Don't forget, it's possible to build both indoors and outdoors, so if the need arises while you're within a large structure, build walls or protective barriers to shield your soldier from incoming gunfire or attacks.

If you're in an inside area where enemies could approach from multiple directions, build stone or metal walls to block one or more of the openings that lead to your location.

While inside large buildings or structures, once you know there are no enemies lurking around, take a few minutes to use your soldier's Harvesting Tool to smash objects and gather resources. Within buildings you'll often find plenty of metal objects, which will allow you to increase your stockpile of metal.

If you suspect that enemies will be following you into large buildings or structures, set Traps in places they won't see as they enter, so you can injure or defeat them without sticking around.

As you approach any building or structure, if it has windows, tiptoe as close as you can from the outside and peek through the window. If you spot enemies, consider shooting them or tossing an explosive weapon through the window. Remember, some explosive weapons (like Dynamite or Grenades) take a few seconds to detonate. However, while Clingers also have a delayed detonation, they stick to their target and can't be removed.

If you're going to toss or shoot a Grenade through a window (or use a similar explosive weapon) remember that these items bounce off of solid objects, so toss or shoot them into a structure, not at one of the structure's walls.

Shown here, a Grenade has been tossed at a solid wall and has bounced back toward the soldier who threw it. A better approach would have been to toss a Grenade through the upstairs window.

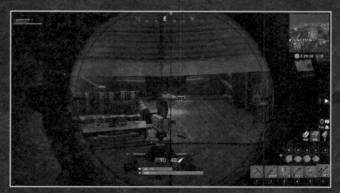

Instead of trying to defeat enemies already in a large structure, one strategy is to grab a long-range weapon with a scope, hide at a safe distance from the entrance, and then shoot at enemies as they exit the structure. You can also toss Stink Bombs through a window of an enclosed space and force enemies to come running out of a structure.

Many large structures on the island contain hidden rooms or basements where you're almost always apt to find useful items to improve your arsenal. You may not be able to see a chest that's hidden, but if you listen carefully, you'll be able to hear the unique sound a chest makes and be able to tell which direction the sound is coming from.

Each gaming season has some type of theme. One of the themes in Season 8, for example, involved pirates. Thus, one of the large structures that could be found on the island was a large pirate ship. It's often within these theme-based buildings or structures where you'll find special weapons or items that are also theme-oriented.

The Pirate Ship, like many themed structures that were temporarily added to the island, contained multiple levels, with many small rooms. Inside these areas lots of loot could be acquired. The trick is for your soldier to be the first person to arrive at each location so they can open the chests and grab what's lying on the ground.

It's within the pirate-themed areas where you were apt to find Cannons which could be ridden around the island just like Shopping Carts or used to shoot cannonballs capable of destroying buildings or structures.

Cannons can shoot cannonballs capable of destroying structures (proper aim is required). They could also be pushed up a hill or mountain and then ridden like a vehicle.

Farmland

You may have heard about the world-famous farmer, named Old McDonald, and all of the adorable animals he has on his lovely farm. Within the farmland found on the island in *Fortnite: Battle Royale*, however, there's nothing cute, like horses, sheep, or chickens. Instead, you'll find potential danger around every cornstalk and haystack.

During Season 8, for example, the name of the largest farmland area on the island continued to be Fatal Fields. In future seasons, this particular area might change, but there will likely always be farmland territory on the

island that offers its own set of challenges and structures. Let's explore how to take full advantage of farmland terrain during your visits to the island.

The layout of the farmland on the mysterious island has changed over time, but the farmland region(s) typically include a large farmhouse, stable, barn, silos, a variety of smaller sheds and buildings, plus large fields (often containing crops) that are unique to this type of terrain.

If your goal is to have your soldier land somewhere in the farmland area after leaping from the Battle Bus, consider landing directly on the roof of the farmhouse.

Once you determine that the farmland area of the island is your desired landing spot, access the Map screen and place a Marker exactly where you'd like to land. When you return to the main game screen, a colored flare (that only you, or you and your partner/squad mates will see) will be visible from the air. It's seen here on the right side of the screen.

To determine the best moment to jump from the Battle Bus, watch the distance marker near the colored flare. As the bus gets closer, the distance meter will count down. The ideal time to jump is at the closest point the Battle Bus comes to the designated landing spot. As soon as you see the distance meter start counting up (meaning you're now moving farther away), this is the perfect time to jump and nosedive toward the landing spot to get there the quickest way possible.

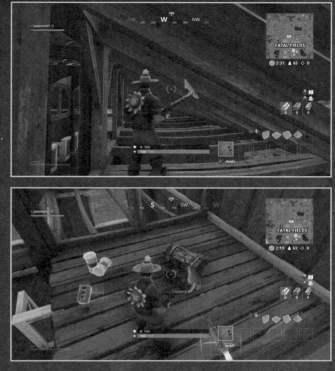

Within the farmhouse, be sure to explore the attic. Like almost any house on the island, you can land on its roof and smash your way through it into the attic using your soldier's Harvesting Tool, or you can enter through the front or back farmhouse door, and then make your way up the stairs. On the top level, build a ramp from the floor to ceiling, and then smash your way through the ceiling to reach the attic.

Another good landing location is right near the front door of the large farmhouse. This multi-level structure always contains several chests, as well as weapons, ammo, and loot items lying out in the open (on the ground).

If you choose to enter the farmhouse on ground level, before entering through the front or back door, sneak up to the building and peek through the windows. Look for signs of enemies inside. Also, stand still for a few moments outside the farmhouse and listen carefully for movement inside. The sounds from enemies walking, running, opening/closing doors, harvesting resources, looting, or participating in close-range firefights will likely be heard if there's potential danger inside.

Especially if you're not yet armed with a weapon, when you open the farmhouse's front or back door, stand to the side in case there's an enemy inside waiting to shoot anyone who enters. If the building (or at least the first floor) seems empty, proceed inside with caution.

One item you'll likely find in the farmhouse, either within a chest or lying on the ground is a Shield Potion. Be sure to grab it. If this is your first stop after landing on the island, or your soldier's Shield meter has not yet been activated or is low, take a few seconds (if it's safe) to drink the Shield Potion to increase your soldier's Shield meter.

On the upper floors of the farmhouse, you'll discover many rooms. If the doors to these rooms are closed, this can mean one of two things. First, that the rooms have not yet been explored and looted by enemies. However, it could also mean that an experienced soldier entered one of the rooms, closed the door behind themselves, and is waiting inside to ambush your soldier. Listen for the sound of movement and be cautious opening each door.

Most of the rooms in the farmhouse resemble rooms found in other houses, buildings, and mansions on the island. On the ground, you'll sometimes find weapons, ammo, and loot items lying on the ground (out in the open), waiting to be grabbed. Pick up items that you want or need. Don't fill up your soldier's inventory with anything you don't anticipate needing or using in the future.

The bathroom of the farmhouse contains a broken wall that leads to a secret room. Inside you'll typically discover a chest, but you'll need to smash through the wall to reach it. Remember, smashing walls makes noise, so if there are enemies in the farmhouse (or directly outside), they'll hear the commotion you make trying to reach this chest.

A large, multi-level barn is another building you'll find in the farmland area.

The barn, along with some of the sheds and other structures in the area, are filled with haystacks. While a soldier can hide behind haystacks to stay out of sight, these offer no shielding protection. One hit from a bullet, and the haystacks will disappear.

Anytime you encounter a pile of tires, jump on them and your soldier will fly into the air. This is a quick and easy way to reach the second level of the barn, for example, without climbing stairs.

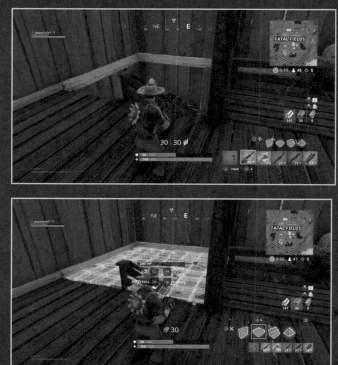

While in the barn (or any building for that matter), after climbing up a staircase, to slow down any enemies that might be following you, build a floor panel out of stone or metal to cover the stairwell. The enemy will first need to bust through the barrier in order to reach you. This will give you a few extra seconds to make an escape or get in the best position for a close-range firefight.

In between the buildings and structures in the farmland area(s), you'll often encounter vast and open spaces. When trying to travel across one of these areas, your soldier will be vulnerable to an attack and will have nothing to hide behind for shielding, unless you quickly build a wall or structure. Driving a vehicle through open spaces allows you to get through those areas faster. Instead of driving in a straight line, drive in an unpredictable, zig-zag pattern. Do the same if you're running on foot.

Never walk or run in a straight line. Travel in a zig-zag pattern and keep jumping. The objective is to be as unpredictable as possible, and to be a moving target that's difficult for your enemies to shoot at.

If you walk up to one of the silos (while standing on the ground), use your soldier's Harvesting Tool to smash them. Not only will this help you to increase your stash of Metal that can be used for building, but upon destroying each Silo, you'll often discover a chest or at least a weapon (with ammo) inside.

The tallest object in the farmland region is not a hill or mountain—it's a pair of metal silos. If you land on top of a silo (after leaping from the Battle Bus or using a Grappler, Balloons, or Launch Pad, for example), you'll get a great view of the surrounding area and can shoot at enemies below.

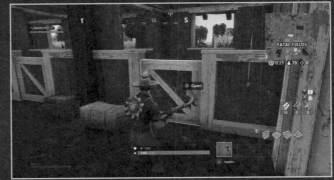

Inside the stables, check each stall by opening its small door. You'll often find weapons, ammo, and/or items lying on the ground waiting to be grabbed. If you step into a stall while armed with a weapon, close the door, crouch down, and hide. When an enemy comes toward you, launch a surprise attack.

Several cornfields with tall crops are placed around the farmland area. It's possible to walk, run, or drive a vehicle through the cornfields, although visibility will be very limited. To see where you are, jump up to peek over the tops of the corn. To destroy the corn and gain Wood, use your Harvesting Tool to harvest the corn as you walk or run through it. Cornfields also offer a great place to hide, if you stand still or crouch down and remain still.

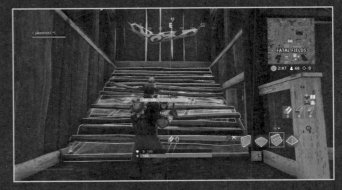

The loft area of the stable often contains a chest. While you might not see the glow from the chest, listen carefully for the sound a chest makes. To reach the loft, build a ramp and then climb up to the loft.

While you're exploring the farmland area of the island, keep in mind that this is typically a popular location, so expect to find multiple enemies lurking around. As you can see, there are plenty of places to hide and launch ambushes from, plus there are many ways to reach a high-up location so you can shoot down toward enemies still on the ground.

Anytime you need to hide or reload your weapon, crouch behind a solid object for cover. Again, don't rely on haystacks to offer any protection whatsoever.

One of the other larger structures you'll find in the farmland area is a stable. It has an entrance on two sides, but you may need to smash them open using your soldier's Harvesting Tool. You can also shoot at the blocked doorways to clear them.

If you enjoy spending time in the farmland area (and with practice get good at defeating enemies in this type of terrain), consider dressing up your soldier in the Hayseed or Sunflower outfit, both of which have a whimsical farming theme.

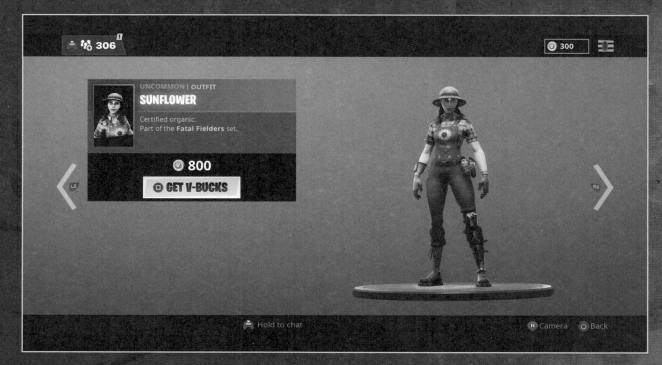

Sunflower is the female version of the Hayseed farmer outfit. Both are sold separately as part of the Fatal Fielders set.

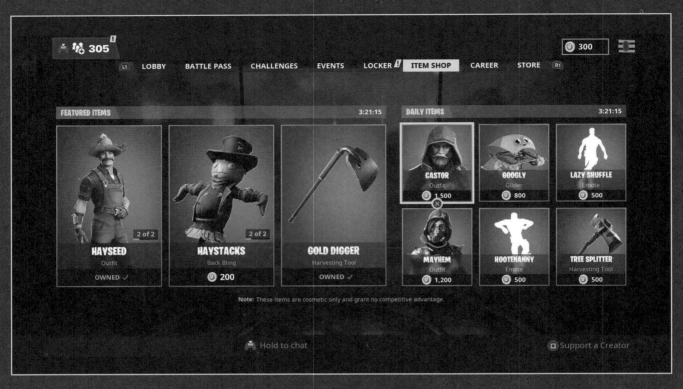

Hayseed and Sunflower have an optional and matching Back Bling and Harvesting Tool design (sold separately). Because these two outfits are classified as Uncommon, they're re-released within Fortnite: Battle Royale's Item Shop periodically and are priced at 800 V-Bucks each (approximately $8.00 US). The Gold Digger Harvesting Tool design is also priced at 800 V-Bucks, while the Sun Sprout or Haystacks Back Bling designs are each priced at 200 V-Bucks (about $2.00 US).

Forests and Tropical Areas

As you've probably guessed, forests and tropical areas contain large trees.

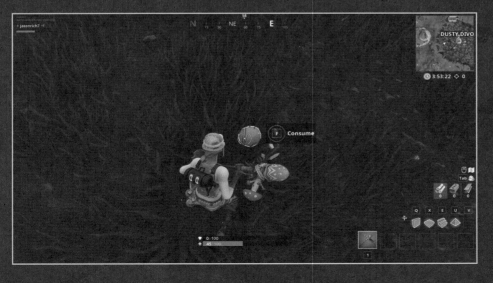

Below some trees, you're apt to find Apples, Mushrooms, or other Health/Shield replenishment items. These items must be grabbed and consumed when and where you find them. Unlike other items, they can't be picked up, stored within your soldier's Inventory, and then used when needed. An Apple, for example, will increase your soldier's Health meter by 5 points. Consuming a Mushroom (shown here) will increase your soldier's Shield meter by 5 points.

As you make your way through a forest area, your soldier can crouch down and hide behind a tree for cover from incoming weapon fire.

It's also possible to stand on the very top of a tree and hide there. This will give you a height advantage if you need to shoot enemies below. Hiding in a tree often offers an obstructed view of your soldier's surroundings. Don't jump from the top of tall trees. The fall could be deadly.

Use a Baller's Grappler to reach the top of the tree and hide there while inside the vehicle. This gives you added protection and shielding, plus allows you to make a quick escape, since you can drop from the tree while in a vehicle and receive no damage.

Trees are also an excellent source for harvesting and collecting wood using your soldier's Harvesting Tool. Just like almost every object on the island, when your soldier faces a tree, that tree's HP meter is displayed. Each time you smash a tree using your soldier's Harvesting Tool, your soldier will collect some wood, but some of the tree's HP meter will also be depleted.

When a tree's HP meter hits zero, that tree will disappear. This can be seen from a distance by your enemies and could reveal your location. To avoid this, keep smashing a tree with the Harvesting Tool until the tree's HP meter gets very low. Before it hits zero (in this case it's at 50HP), stop smashing and move to another tree. By doing this, the tree will remain standing.

As you explore a forest, keep your eye out for weapons, ammo, loot items, and even chests that may be lying on the ground, either out in the open, or that are semi-hidden near the trunk of a tree.

The small structures found within forest areas sometimes contain useful items.

If the structure needs more protection, build a wall. Then take the time to rearrange your soldier's Inventory or consume Health or Shield replenishment items, as needed.

Of course, if you have enough resources at your disposal, building a ramp is always a viable option for traveling up and down mountains. Remember, when building a tall ramp, you always run the risk of an enemy destroying just one low-down tile and having the entire ramp collapse with you still on it.

Hills, Cliffs, and Tall Mountains

Throughout the island are hills, cliffs, and mountains. These can be used to give you a height advantage over your enemies or used in other ways to provide a tactical or defensive advantage.

Some hills or mountains have windy pathways to follow that will allow your soldier to easily navigate to the top. An easier way to reach the top of a hill or mountain is to use a vehicle and drive straight up, or use another transportation tool (such as a Launch Pad, Grappler, or Balloons) that'll help your soldier to go airborne and then land at the top of the raised terrain.

Consider building a ramp along the side of a mountain, like the one shown here, as opposed to a bridge that faces toward the mountain. Once you reach the top of a ramp, if you don't think you'll need to use it again, destroy it so an enemy can't easily follow you to your location without building their own ramp.

From the top of a hill or mountain, you'll typically have a great view of the surrounding area and will be able to see enemies approaching from all directions. If the mountaintop isn't high enough, don't forget you can easily build a ramp, fortress, or structure on the mountaintop to gain height and visibility, as well as protective shielding. Some hills and mountaintops already have a structure placed there. Be sure to explore these structures and look for useful goodies to collect that'll improve your soldier's arsenal.

Anytime you suspect an enemy is above you, consider building an over-under ramp that includes a roof that'll provide protection from overhead attacks as you're traveling up or down. To create this type of ramp, point the building cursor directly ahead of your soldier, as opposed to near your soldier's feet as he's moving forward and simultaneously building ramp tiles.

Keep an eye out for vehicles on top of hills and mountains. These can provide an easy way for getting down quickly and safely. Another option is to use an item, such as a Launch Pad or Balloons, that'll help your soldier go airborne and then land safely back on the ground.

Unless you're in a vehicle, never jump off the side of a mountain or cliff. The fall will result in an inujry or could defeat your soldier instantly. In many situations, however, you're able to slide down the side of a mountain and reach the ground safely.

At the end of a zipline's route, a soldier will safely land. However, by pressing the Jump button/key while your soldier is riding a zipline, you can make them exit the zipline at any time. Don't do this while he is high up, or he'll fall to his death.

During your soldier's freefall at the start of a match, look for weapons or chests on the top of hills or mountains, and consider those as potential landing locations. Landing on an elevated location offers a height advantage, and if you know you'll be able to quickly grab a weapon, that's even better.

During the End Game, for example, if the circle permits, try to reach the top of a hill or mountain and build a fortress on top. This allows you to see enemies approaching from any direction and gives you a height advantage.

At the top and bottom of some mountains, you may encounter ziplines. These provide an easy way to get from one location to another, as long as the path you need to take follows the zipline route. Keep in mind, you cannot destroy a zipline or the red bars that support ziplines.

Soldiers riding a zipline can be shot, although they're typically a moving target. The soldier that's riding the zipline can also use a weapon.

It's possible to control your soldier's movement along the zipline and quickly switch traveling directions or come to a complete stop. You're also able to twist your soldier's body around while in motion in order to look around and shoot in various directions.

Lakes and Rivers

On foot, a faster and safer way to travel across a body of water is to build a bridge using wood.

Up until near the end of Season 8, Loot Lake was a popular water-filled area, but like everything else on the island, this too has changed. There are, however, plenty of other lakes and water-based areas to contend with, regardless of which gaming season you're experiencing. This is what Loot Lake looked like as Season 8 started to wind down and a new mysterious change began taking place.

As your soldier is crossing the bridge, if someone starts shooting, you're able to build a small fortress or barrier to provide shielding.

If you're the driver in most vehicle types, you cannot drive and build at the same time. However, if your vehicle has a passenger, that soldier can build a bridge while you're driving (or vice versa).

In general, any time you choose to travel through water without using a vehicle, especially if it's deep water, it's going to slow your soldier down. Doing this will also typically leave your soldier out in the open and vulnerable to attack. If your soldier is in the middle of a lake, for example, he can't start building. He can, however, use an item or weapon.

Having your soldier make could with water is not a problem. However, there are certain types of liquid, such as lava or toxic waste, that injure your soldier if they touch it molten hot lava.

Depending on the gaming season, some bodies of water on the island may be frozen solid, so your soldier can walk or drive right over them. Once your soldier's feet are exposed to the icy surface of a lake for too long, their feet will transform into ice blocks, and they'll be able to slide along the surface quickly and over great distances. While you will have less precise control than when walking or running, having ice blocks on your soldier's feet allows for faster movement without a vehicle.

Geysers are randomly occurring natural phenomenon that occur on the island. When your soldier steps into a Geyser, they'll go airborne. Use the directional controls to navigate. Your soldier's Glider will automatically deploy to ensure a safe landing.

A hoverboard, for example, travels over the surface of water, so you won't be slowed down, regardless of how deep the water is.

Junkyards and Storage Container Facilities Can Also Often Be Found on the Island

While exploring these areas, smashing vehicles, cargo containers, or other types of junk using your soldier's Harvesting Tool will allow you to collect resources, but you'll make a lot of noise in the process.

The ground level of these areas is like a maze with lots of sharp turns that you can't see around. If an enemy is above you and you're stuck on the ground, you'll definitely be at a disadvantage in terms of being able to see what's around, as well as your ability to shoot at enemies above you.

During just about every gaming season thus far, the island has included at least one (usually several) junk yards and/or storage container facilities.

The easiest way to give yourself a tactical advantage in these areas is to stay as high up as possible. Climb on top of a car, junk, or cargo container pile so you can shoot at enemies below and get a better view of the whole area. Either that or stay on the roof of a building that overlooks the area. A third option is to build your own reinforced ramp to get your soldier as high up as possible.

If you must stay on ground level, move slowly and keep your weapon drawn. While you may encounter enemies on ground level with you, they're probably newbs. The more advanced players will be attacking from above. One way to injure or eliminate your enemies on ground level in this type of terrain is to place Traps. Shown here, there's a Trap placed on the roof of a small chamber ahead. This Trap would work better, however, if it were more strategically placed and could not be seen as easily.

Look for chests, as well as weapons, ammo, and loot items to be lying on top of vehicle, junk, or cargo container piles, as well as on ground level, and within the buildings that surround these areas. As always, before you start looting, make sure the area is clear of enemies.

Since these areas contain a lot of sharp turns, where you can't see what's around the bend, proceed with caution and listen carefully for the movement of enemies, since you'll typically hear them before you see them.

Narrow Tunnels (Mines, Caves, and Pyramids)

Various areas of the island, such as within underground mines, inside caves, or while exploring pyramids, for example, will require your soldier to navigate through narrow tunnels that often contain sharp turns or windy routes. Anytime you're traveling through this type of terrain, have a close-range weapon (such as a Pistol) drawn and ready to fire. To make the least amount of noise possible, have your soldier crouch down while walking.

While exploring underground areas, always be on the lookout for hidden rooms or chambers. These often contain chests or other items that are well worth collecting. Look for changes in the walls or sounds from behind walls to determine where hidden chambers are located, and then use the Harvesting Tool to smash through them.

If you suspect an enemy is hiding out around a bend, try tossing an explosive weapon or Stink Bomb, for example, in their direction. Either that or be ready to fire your gun as soon as you make the turn around a bend.

Consider dropping one or two powerful weapons or loot items at the intersection area of two or more tunnels, so these items can easily be seen from all directions. Next, hide in one of the tunnels, but keep your weapon aimed at the items you've chosen to use for bait. As soon as an enemy approaches the items you've dropped, start shooting. In small and enclosed areas like mines or cave tunnels, for example, this is often more effective than placing a Trap.

As always, anytime you can maintain a height advantage over your potential enemies during a firefight, the better off you'll be. When searching through tunnels of a mine, cave, or pyramid, for example, look for an object or area you can climb to get up higher than ground level, so you can aim downward at your targets when shooting.

Use blind turns and narrow bottlenecks to your advantage. By positioning your soldier in the right place, you'll be able to aim and fire at enemies the moment they become visible. Try to pre-aim the gun's targeting sights exactly where you anticipate your enemy appearing, so you're ready to fire the moment they are spotted.

Just as in any close-range fighting situation, the best weapons to use include any type of Pistol, although a Legendary-rated Hand Cannon is particularly powerful.

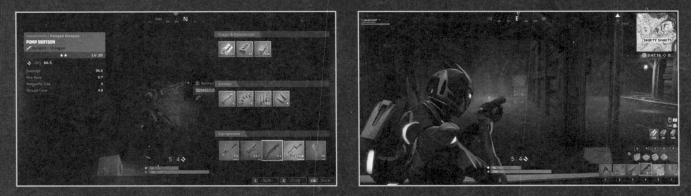

A Pump Shotgun can also pack a wallop at close range and is often preferred over any type of Pistol for close-range firefights. Another good weapon option is an SMG or Compact SMG when you're engaged in gun battles within buildings, structures, mines, or anywhere indoors.

Depending on the type of close-range weapon you're using, make sure you have a good supply of ammo on hand. Most Pistols and SMGs use Light Bullets, while Shotguns use Shells (shown here). Some of the ways to gather ammo include finding it lying on the ground, within chests, as well as within Ammo Boxes, Loot Llamas, and Supply Drops. You can also collect the ammo that an enemy soldier was carrying once they've been defeated and eliminated from a match.

Random Small Structures and Outposts

Scattered throughout the island, primarily in between the labeled points of interest on the map, you'll find many small structures during every match.

Some of the smaller structures you'll encounter are theme oriented, based on what's happening during the current gaming season of Fortnite: Battle Royale.

As you make your way between points of interest, some of these structures offer a good place to rest and hide out for a few minutes, so you can use Health and/or Shield replenishment items with a lower risk of getting attacked while your soldier is vulnerable.

Within some structures, you'll discover weapons, ammo, and/or loot items lying on the ground your soldier can grab. In this structure, the glow from the chest was visible from the outside.

Once the soldier was temporarily safe, he took the time to drink a Slurp Juice.

Small structures located in between points of interest are also good stopping points if you need to access your soldier's Inventory screen and rearrange their arsenal. Once again, these buildings often offer a safe sanctuary. Look for a stone structure (because it's sturdy and can withstand an attack for longer), that has a no windows and just one door. This offers the most protection.

Once safely inside a structure, access your soldier's Inventory screen and move things around in his/her arsenal, if necessary.

Another way you can use small structures to your tactical advantage is to set Traps within them, and then drop one or two useful loot items someplace where your enemies will see them. These items will serve as bait. Once they enter into the structure, the Trap will activate, and you'll inflict damage without actually being there.

If you encounter a hut that's raised and another soldier has already built a ramp to the doorway, you know that anything that might have been inside has already been taken. There's also a chance that the enemy is still camped out inside the small structure. When it's your soldier hanging out in one of these structures, be sure to destroy the ramp after you climb up it, to cover your tracks.

These small crypts make great hiding places, because there is only one entrance, no windows, and the structures are made of stone. Often you'll also find something worth grabbing inside. As always, watch for the glow of a chest.

Lonely Lodge is one of the camping areas that's been a point of interest on the island for many gaming seasons. Other camping areas come and go. In addition to coming across tents and lodges, you'll see these small log cabins scattered about.

Once inside one of these small log cabins, crouch down and guard the door, so you're ready to attack an enemy who enters. You can also take a minute to use Health or Shield replenishment items you're carrying, check or rearrange your soldier's inventory (from the Inventory screen), or place one or two Traps within the cabin that'll surprise the next soldier who enters once you leave.

Seasonal Themed Areas

The seasonal themed areas or structures that get introduced to the island tend to be unique each season. It might be a massive military base, a pirate ship, a Viking ship stuck on the top of a mountain, a mansion on top of a mountain, or a giant volcano, for example.

Whatever the special theme areas are during the current gaming season, you can be sure that they'll be popular landing destinations at the start of each match. So, if you choose to land at one of these locations, expect a lot of company and be ready for battle within moments of landing.

Another thing you can be sure about when visiting one of these themed locations is that it'll be chock full of chests, weapons, ammo, and often rare loot items—that is, if you're the first soldier to reach the area to grab what's there.

In recent gaming seasons, each time Epic Games has introduced a new themed area or structure onto the island, it's also contained specialty weapons, vehicles, and/or other transportation methods that are initially unique to that area. In this case, Frosty Flights used to be an airport where X-4 Stormwing airplanes could be found. During a later gaming season, within the airplane hangars you'd find multiple Ballers.

While X-4 Stormwing airplanes were vaulted for Solo, Duo, and Squads matches, they are occasionally re-introduced into the game. For example, this Air Royale temporary game play mode was all about participating in airborne battles and piloting the planes with a partner who stood on the wing shooting at enemies.

Instead of landing directly within a popular themed area at the start of a match, until you get to know the new territory, consider landing in the outskirts of the area. This will give you added time to grab a weapon and establish your soldier's arsenal before you encounter enemies and are forced into a battle.

As always, based on the type of terrain you're in, choose an appropriate weapon. Anytime you're indoors or in a confined area, a close-range weapon will serve you well. When in a more open area, choose the most powerful mid-range weapon you can get your hands on, and that you're most proficient using.

Don't get distracted by the new scenery when visiting a themed area, especially near the beginning of a new gaming season. Don't forget that your soldier's aim will always be better if they're crouching down and not moving, but they'll also have good aim if they're standing upright, but still. Any movement while aiming a weapon—whether it involves walking, running, tiptoeing, riding within a vehicle that allows your soldier to use a weapon, or while riding a zipline, for example—will reduce your soldier's aiming accuracy, regardless of which weapon they're using.

Suburban Areas with Homes and Mansions

There are multiple regions on the island that offer suburban areas, with clusters of homes located relatively close together. Other regions have mansions, which are larger homes, and that are more spread out.

As you travel between labeled points of interest on the map, you're apt to discover individual homes randomly scattered throughout the island.

While you'll likely find weapons, ammo, and loot items lying on the ground, out in the open when exploring homes, the good stuff can of often be found in the house's attic or basement.

One way to reach a house's attic is to go inside and make your way to the top floor.

Build a ramp from the floor to the ceiling.

Another way to reach a house's attic is to build a ramp from the outside.

Use your soldier's Harvesting Tool to smash through the ceiling and gain access to the attic.

To reach the roof of a house from the outside, you can also use an item, such as a Launch Pad, Grappler, or Balloons, that'll help your soldier go airborne. When leaping from the Battle Bus at the start of a match, you can always opt to land on a house's roof.

In many attics (but not all of them) you'll discover a chest, or other things worth grabbing.

Once you're on a house's roof, use your Harvesting Tool to smash your way through the roof and then jump down into the attic.

Not all houses contain basements. When they do, you can either reach it by going inside and taking the stairs downward, or from the outside, look for cellar doors on the ground. Smash or shoot open one of the cellar doors and go inside.

While inside a house, if you encounter enemies, you'll likely need to engage in close-range combat, so have an appropriate weapon ready. From the top of a staircase is often a good place to engage an enemy as they're climbing up the stairs.

Before entering a house, look and listen carefully for signs that someone may already be inside. For example, if you see the front or back door wide open, this indicates someone has already been inside. Anytime you enter into a house or enter into a room within a house and need to open a door, proceed with caution. You never know what could be waiting on the opposite side.

One way to defeat enemies is to place various types of Traps inside the house, near an entrance or near a staircase, so an enemy will accidently walk into the Trap and activate it before they spot it.

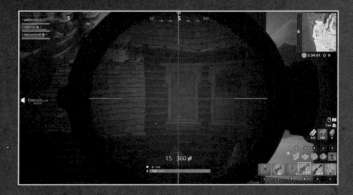

In a suburban area where houses are close together, you can go to the second floor of one house, aim through a window, and then use a Sniper Rifle (or another weapon with a scope) to shoot at enemies coming or going from a nearby house. Aiming for the front door gives you time to position yourself and aim your weapon. Then just wait for the door to open and start shooting whomever is coming or going.

Remember, from the outside of a house, you can shoot at enemies through windows or an open door. You can also toss explosive weapons, like Grenades, Dynamite, or Clingers through an open door or window to cause some destruction.

While exploring a house, this is a good time to use the Harvesting Tool to smash objects and collect resources. Smash walls, floors, ceilings, furniture, or appliances, for example. However, anytime you're inside of a house, your soldier will make noise when walking, running, harvesting resources, opening/closing doors, building, or firing a weapon. If someone else is in the house, they'll be able to tell where you are, based on where the noise is coming from.

Don't forget, you're able to build inside or outside of an existing house, building, or structure. Here, a three-level fortress (made from wood and stone) was built on the roof of a house. From the top of this fortress, the soldier can look out and see the entire neighborhood. When using a Sniper Rifle (or any weapon with a scope), it's easy to target the door of another house and wait for an enemy to enter or exit so you can shoot them.

Block Off Stairwells After Climbing Up

Once you've climbed up a staircase to reach a higher floor of a building, slow down enemies that may be following you by building walls to block the staircase.

In this case, first a brick floor tile was built over the staircase.

Next, a brick pyramid tile was built on top of the floor tile.

Finally, a brick wall was built as a third blockade to keep enemies from easily following the soldier into the building. Once this is done, if you hear an enemy approaching, make your way to a safe location (to avoid possible explosions), crouch down, and get ready for the enemy to breach your barrier. Either that or make a quick exit by building a bridge out of a window, for example.

Urban Areas with Tall Buildings

Since *Fortnite: Battle Royale* first launched, Tilted Towers (located near map coordinates D5.5) has been one of the game's most popular points of interest. Sure, it's changed and evolved over time, but this urban area is filled with tall buildings, streets, shops, a parking lot, a tall clock tower, and plenty of structures to explore. At any given time, this is just one of the urban areas you'll discover on the island.

Urban areas tend to be the most popular on the island, so you're virtually guaranteed to encounter a bunch of enemies right away, so be prepared!

General Strategies for Exploring and Fighting in and Around Buildings

If you choose to land in an urban area, your landing spot should be on the roof of a tall building or structure. Either look for the glow of a chest on the roof, or at least the glare or reflection from a weapon that's lying on the roof, out in the open.

Land and grab a weapon right away! As you can see here, the soldier was able to grab a Pistol. She's now able to defend herself when an enemy lands right after her, or she encounters rivals as she explores the building she landed on.

When exploring an urban area with tall buildings that are located relatively close to each other, one strategy for survival is to stick to the high ground. Find and grab a long-range weapon, and then pick off enemies by peeking out a window from a high-up floor or the roof of a building.

Instead of walking along the roads or sidewalks (on ground level) within a dense urban area where enemies will often be above you, or could attack from any side, consider traveling quickly (and with great maneuverability) using a Hoverboard. Other vehicles can work too. You might not be able to outrun an incoming attack on foot, but you can often maneuver around quick enough to avoid harm if you're using a vehicle.

If you're riding a Hoverboard in an area with lots of buildings and narrow streets and you attempt to use its Boost feature, you'll have less time to make sharp turns and are more likely to crash into objects or buildings, which will actually slow you down. Ideally, you want to travel as fast as possible, while maintaining control so you can maneuver quickly.

Within many of the buildings, you'll discover chests. As long as it's safe to do so, approach each chest and grab the loot that's inside, so you can build up or improve your soldier's arsenal of weapons and items.

Always be on the lookout for Ammo Boxes. They don't glow or make a sound like chests, but when you open one, you'll be able to stock up on ammo. It's within Ammo Boxes that you'll often find Rockets (which are rarer than other types of ammo).

The guns available on the island use either Light Bullets, Medium Bullets, Heavy Bullets, Shells, or Rockets. If you don't have the right ammo for the guns in your soldier's arsenal, those weapons are useless. Meanwhile, if you run out of ammo during a firefight, or don't swap weapons fast enough, you'll likely wind up getting defeated by your enemy. It's always good to stock up on ammo!

After opening a doorway and passing through, be sure to close the door behind your soldier. An open door is a sure indication someone has been in that area before you. If the door is shut, someone entering after you won't know if you're already inside or not, unless they can hear the sounds your soldier is making.

Avoid getting yourself stuck in a room within a building with no escape plan. In this situation, you'll need to fight your way out. Make sure the door is shut, crouch down behind a solid object (in this case a desk), and aim your weapon at the door. As soon as an enemy tries to enter, start shooting. Just make sure you can't be seen from a window that's behind you or to the sides of you, or a sniper might take you out while you're guarding the door.

Always listen carefully for the sound of footsteps, doors opening and closing, construction noises, and the sound of gunfire. You can often hear enemies approaching before you can see them, especially when you're inside of a building or within a confined space.

As you're exploring a building, crouch down and tiptoe while inside, and always keep your weapon drawn. This will generate much less noise (from footsteps) than walking or running.

If you don't see an enemy right away, focus in on a chest, for example. As soon as an enemy approaches the chest to open it, shoot and try for a headshot.

A headshot always causes more damage than a body shot. Depending on the power and capabilities of the weapon you're using, a single headshot will typically eliminate your adversary.

By climbing to a higher floor in a building, you can look out of a window and use a Sniper Rifle (or any weapon with a scope) to zoom in on an enemy lurking within another building. You'll often see them by peeking through their building's window.

Anytime you need to travel on street level in a city or urban area, avoid being out in the open, in the middle of the street. This makes you an easy target for enemies located above you, as well as those hiding on the ground level in shops or buildings, or behind vehicles or objects, for example. Try to hug a nearby wall, crouch down, and make your soldier the smallest target possible.

Whenever it's necessary, crouch down and hide behind solid objects, like furniture, walls, or broken-down vehicles to shield yourself from enemy attacks. Keep in mind, in an urban area, an attack can come from any direction, including above you.

To escape from a closed-in space on a high-up floor within a building, climb through a nearby window, or smash the outer wall of a building, and then create a ramp or bridge to help you reach safety.

Anytime you're within a building and need to fight an enemy, use a close-range weapon, such as any type of Pistol or Shotgun. An SMG (Submachine Gun) can also do mega-damage at close- to mid-range. SMGs are often a weapon of choice for newbs who need a close-range weapon that's more forgiving and versatile.

Whenever possible, try to have the height advantage over your opponent. This might mean climbing up on furniture, a staircase, or leaning over a ledge, for example. It's almost always easier to accurately target an enemy that's positioned below you.

Never Just Jump Off of a Roof!

Never just leap off of a tall building. If your soldier winds up falling two or three levels, he'll get injured. A fall from above three levels will cause him to perish instantly and with a splat. To get back down to ground level, have your soldier smash through the floor and drop down one level at a time.

Build Bridges to Travel Between Buildings

If you need to travel between buildings, instead of going back to ground level, going outside, and walking (or running) on the sidewalk or street, consider building a bridge between building rooftops. This allows you to stay high up. As you're building or crossing the bridge, run (don't walk), since you'll be out in the open and vulnerable.

Other options for safely reaching ground level include using a Glider item, using Balloons, a Bouncer Pad, or using a Launch Pad (shown here), although not all of these items may be available during your match, as various items often get vaulted and then re-released into the game at a future date. When you go airborne using any of these items, your soldier will not get injured upon landing.

If you've collected a Glider item, for example, and you need to jump from a high-up location back to ground level, first select the Glider that's stored in your soldier's inventory. Next, jump up, and while in midair, activate the Glider. Perfect timing is essential! (This maneuver will likely take some practice.) The Glider will activate, and your soldier will be able to soar through the air and make it safely to the ground. While in the air, use the directional controls to navigate. At this point, the Glider works exactly the same way as it does during your soldier's freefall off of the Battle Bus at the start of each match.

Assuming you have the resources to spare, consider building walls on either side of your bridge that connects two buildings together. Plus, if there are other buildings that are taller in the area, consider adding a roof to the bridge to protect from overhead attacks. This bridge is made of wood. If you anticipate it needing to withstand an attack, build it from stone or metal.

Here's what the bridge (with walls) looks like from below. It offers pretty good protection when traveling between buildings. Once you cross the bridge, if you don't anticipate needing to make a return trip in the other direction, consider destroying it so if an enemy wants to follow, they'll need to use their own resources to build their own bridge.

Anytime you're building bridges, ramps, or structures during a *Fortnite: Battle Royale* match, using wood is always the fastest, but it's also the weakest against attacks. Thus, wood is great for ramps and bridges that won't need to withstand a gunfire or explosive attack.

Stone offers more protection and a higher HP per tile than wood, but it's a bit slower to build with. Metal is definitely the strongest building material. It can offer the greatest level of protection against gunfire or an explosive attack, but it's also the slowest to build with.

One way to travel around this urban area is to hop into s Slipstream and ride within the flowing air tunnel.

Wide-Open Areas with Mostly Flat Terrain

You're going to encounter wide-open areas within many of the labeled points of interest on the island, as well as when you're traveling in between the points of interest.

As you're exploring the island, typically in between labeled points of interest, you'll sometimes stumble upon a campsite. While you might find one or two worthwhile items to pick up that are lying on the ground, in this case, there's an unlit campfire near a small log cabin. The soldier's Health meter is currently very low.

Whenever possible, use your surroundings (such as a rock formation) as cover. If you're in a pinch and bullets are flying toward you, you always have the option of quickly building a barrier or mini-fortress for protection and from which you can more safely launch your own attacks.

Walk up to the Campfire and light it. For every second your soldier stands near the flames, their Health meter will get a boost. This will continue until the flames burn out.

Anytime you need a quick place to hide, try crouching down within (not behind) a nearby bush. This offers no protection against attacks if you're spotted, but if the bush is large enough, it'll keep you from being seen by your enemies.

During the End Game, when the safe area of the island is very small, some gamers opt to hide their soldiers within bushes. So, if you can't locate an enemy that you know is close by, try shooting or tossing explosives into the nearby bushes.

Expect the Unexpected!

Now that you know what to expect from the different types of terrain when exploring the island during each match, there's another extremely important thing you need to take into account—the actions of your adversaries.

Each soldier you encounter on the island is being controlled, in real time, by another gamer. They might be a newb, or they could be one of the highest-ranking *Fortnite: Battle Royale* gamers in the world—you just don't know who you're dealing with until you meet up with them on the island and see their soldier in action.

Whenever you encounter an enemy (or enemies), don't expect them to use common sense or be predictable when reacting to your attack or ambush, for example. Every gamer has their own unique fighting style and defensive strategies, and some have had much less practice than others when playing *Fortnite: Battle Royale*. As a result, expect the unexpected and be ready for anything.

Likewise, when controlling your own soldier during a match, try to be as unpredictable as possible in your movements and actions. If your enemies can't figure out what you're going to do next, they can't prepare to defend themselves against it. Be spontaneous and use the terrain around you to your utmost advantage.

SECTION 4

SURVIVE USING WEAPONS, LOOT ITEMS, AND TOOLS

Winning matches is all about knowing where to find the best weapons, adding the right selection of weapons to your arsenal, and then using the most appropriate weapon for the combat situation you're currently facing. During any single match, you'll likely need to switch between close-range, mid-range, and long-range combat and shooting tactics multiple times in order to defeat your enemies. You'll often benefit from using explosives (or projectile explosive weapons), when appropriate, especially if you need to destroy structures and blow up enemies at the same time.

Building Your Soldier's Arsenal

When it comes to working with weapons during a match, you'll consistently need to use six essential skills, including:

1. Finding weapons and then adding the best selection of them to your soldier's arsenal. The weapons you collect get stored within your soldier's backpack. It only has slots for up to five weapons and/or loot items (excluding your soldier's Harvesting Tool, which can also be used as a short-range weapon).

2. Choosing the most appropriate weapon based on each combat situation. This means quickly analyzing the challenges and rivals you're currently facing, and selecting a close-range, mid-range, or long-range gun, an explosive weapon, or a projectile explosive weapon that'll help you get the job done.

3. Collecting and stockpiling the different types of ammunition and making sure you have an ample supply of ammunition for each weapon you want to use.

4. Positioning yourself in the ideal location, with direct line-of-sight to your target(s), so you can inflict damage in the most accurate and efficient way possible. Headshots always cause more damage than a body shot, for example, when you're targeting enemies.

5. Aim each type of weapon, so you're able to consistently hit your targets, without wasting ammunition or increasing the risk of your enemies having time to shoot back. When your soldier crouches down while shooting a weapon, their aim will always improve. Having to walk or run while shooting reduces your soldier's accuracy when aiming a weapon, but this is often necessary.

6. Shooting the active weapon your soldier is holding, and then quickly switching between weapons as needed.

Once you get good at performing each of these tasks, it'll still take a lot of practice to become a highly skilled sharpshooter who is capable of using single shots to defeat enemies. Plus, you'll need to discover how to best use the weapons at your disposal to destroy structures and fortresses in which your enemies may be hiding.

Most Weapon Types Are Available in Different Tiers

Each weapon type falls into a specific weapon category but is also ranked based on its tier. *Fortnite: Battle Royale* offers weapons that come in several different, color-coded weapon tiers, which impacts their capabilities and ratings. Not all weapon types, however, are available in each of these tiers.

A **Common** version of a weapon has a gray hue and is the weakest.

Weapons with a purple hue, like this Minigun, are considered **Epic**.

An **Uncommon** version of a weapon has a green hue and is slightly more powerful than a Common version of that same weapon.

The most powerful tier of weapons is classified as **Legendary**. These have a golden (orange) hue. These are powerful weapons that are the hardest to find. Shown here is a Legendary Rocket Launcher that was acquired from a Vending Machine. This is one of the most powerful projectile explosive weapons available. It can be used to destroy structures or objects from a distance. When the Aim feature is used, targeting is very precise.

Understand How Weapons Are Rated

Every weapon offered within *Fortnite: Battle Royale* is rated based on several criteria. Combined, this determines how much damage a direct hit from that weapon can cause, based on certain situations. For example, a headshot will always cause more damage than a body shot when shooting at enemies.

A **Rare** weapon has a blue hue, which is a bit more powerful than an Uncommon version of that same weapon.

Likewise, when you shoot at a structure, as opposed to an enemy soldier, the amount of damage each direct hit causes will be different.

Each weapon is rated based on its:

Damage Per Second (DPS) Rating—This determines how much damage a weapon can cause per second of continuous firing.

Damage Rating—This is a measure of how much overall damage the weapon can cause per direct hit.

Fire Rate—This determines how many rounds or bullets can be fired per second, either using a Continuous or Burst shooting mode, or by quickly pressing the trigger.

Magazine (Mag) Size—Each weapon can hold a pre-determined number of bullets or rounds of ammunition at once before it needs to be reloaded. The Mag Size shows you the maximum number of bullets/rounds that can be held by the weapon at once.

Reload Time—This determines how long it takes to reload the weapon once the magazine is empty. During this time, your soldier becomes vulnerable to attack and can't shoot back at their enemies. Some of the most powerful weapons in *Fortnite: Battle Royale* offer a small magazine size and slow reload time, but each direct hit causes the most damage on your target. A weapon with a fast reload time might have a smaller Mag Size or use less-powerful ammo.

Structure Damage—This is a measure of how much damage a direct hit will cause on a structure, object, or building (as opposed to a soldier).

Some weapons allow you to choose between multiple firing modes. The **Single** fire mode means that one bullet is fired each time the weapon's trigger is pulled. When a weapon uses a **Burst** firing mode, multiple rounds of ammo are fired each time the trigger is pulled.

Using **Continuous** fire mode, bullets keep firing continuously as long as you hold down the weapon's trigger or until the weapon runs out of ammo. Keep in mind that not all weapons allow you to switch between firing modes.

Don't forget, every type of gun requires compatible ammo. There are different types of ammo to find and stockpile. It's essential that you maintain an ample supply of ammo for the specific weapons you're carrying.

Light Bullets are typically used in smaller, hand-held weapons, such as Pistols and some SMGs.

Medium Bullets cause more damage than Light Bullets. These are typically used with Assault Rifles and work particularly well when used at mid-range.

Heavy Bullets are used mainly in Sniper Rifles. This are the highest caliber ammo available on the island, and useful for reaching long-range targets. Weapons that use Heavy Bullets tend to have a low fire rate and long

reload time but cause the most damage per shot when a direct hit is made.

Rockets are a projectile and explosive type of ammo that get shot from a Rocket Launcher, Quad Launcher, Grenade Launcher, "Boom Bow" or Guided Missile Launcher, for example. This type of ammo can be shot from a distance, and then explodes upon impact. Not only is it useful for inflicting major damage on enemies, it can also be used to easily and quickly destroy structures or objects.

Shells are used in various types of Shotguns. These weapons work well against close- to mid-range targets for a few reasons. For example, when a shell is shot from a Shotgun, the ammo splits apart into many tiny pieces. When those pieces hit one target, each piece of the shrapnel causes a lot of damage. However, if two targets are at close range, pieces from a single shell can hit and injure (or even defeat) multiple targets at once.

The drawback to a Shotgun that shoots Shells is that if you're too far away from your target when shooting this weapon, the Shell fragments have time to spread out a lot. Less of the ammo will hit your intended target, which means each hit causes much less damage. Plus, the farther away you are from your target when using a Shotgun, the less accurate your aim will be.

Remember, Ammo Boxes provide an excellent way to restock your soldier's ammo. These boxes don't glow or make a sound like chests, but when you open one, you'll be able to stock up on ammo. It's within Ammo Boxes that you'll often find Rockets (which are rarer than other types of ammo).

The guns available on the island use either Light Bullets, Medium Bullets, Heavy Bullets, Shells, or Rockets. If you don't have the right ammo for the guns in your soldier's arsenal, those weapons are useless. Meanwhile, if you run out of ammo during a firefight, or don't swap weapons fast enough, you'll likely wind up getting defeated by your enemy. It's always good to stock up on ammo!

Learn to Switch Weapons Quickly

Either as you prepare for a firefight or while in the middle of one, there will be many times during a match when you must quickly switch between active weapons and items, or switch between Combat mode and Building mode. This is a skill that'll take practice.

Combat modes give you full access to your weapons, loot items, and anything else in your soldier's inventory. When in Building mode, your soldier can use the resources they have collected (wood, stone, and metal) to build structures and fortresses. While in Building mode, however, no weapons can be used.

On most gaming systems, displayed in the bottom-right corner of the main game screen is a summary of your soldier's main inventory. Each of the slots represents one weapon or item your soldier is carrying. The left-most slot typically contains the Harvesting Tool. This cannot be dropped.

You have full control over the six remaining inventory slots. As you find and grab weapons and loot items, pick and choose what you want to carry and have available, and then from the Inventory screen, re-arrange the order of the items as needed.

Some gamers opt to place their favorite type of gun in the slot to the immediate right of the Harvesting tool (the slot on the extreme left). They use the next one or two slots for their next most commonly used weapons, and then insert one or two loot items (such as a Health or Shield replenishment item) in the right-most inventory slots. (A slot for the Harvesting tool is displayed on some gaming systems, but not others.)

From the Inventory screen, use the Move or Drop commands to rearrange what's in each Inventory slot as needed.

During firefights, keep your eye on the amount of ammo within the gun you're using. Each weapon takes a different amount of time to reload, during which time you cannot fire that weapon. Knowing that you'll need to reload your weapon, choose a place you can duck behind for protection, such as behind a barrier or wall.

To speed up the time it takes once a weapon needs to be reloaded, consider having a duplicate weapon in the Inventory slot next to the one you're using. When one gun needs to be reloaded, simply switch to the other one. There will still be a small amount of time where you can't shoot, but the time will often be shorter than reloading the one weapon.

How to Rearrange What's in Inventory Slots

Whenever you pick up a new weapon or loot item, it automatically gets placed within an available Inventory slot. Your soldier's Inventory slots initially fill up from left to right.

However, during a match, it's a good strategy to rearrange the items in your inventory so your most powerful and frequently used weapons and items are placed in the left-most slots. To rearrange what's in your Inventory slots, follow these steps:

1. Access your soldier's Inventory screen.
2. Highlight and select one of the items you want to move.
3. On a PC, drag the item from one Inventory slot to another. On a console-based system, select the Move command, and then position the cursor over the slot you want to move the selected item to.

In most situations, it makes little or no sense to carry around two of the same weapon, since inventory space is limited, and you want to have a well-rounded selection of weapons available.

One instance when you might want to carry duplicate weapons is if you have a favorite weapon that has a small Magazine Size and slow Reload Time. By placing the two identical weapons in inventory slots directly next to each other, instead of waiting for one weapon to reload when it runs out of ammo, you can quickly switch to the other (identical weapon) and keep firing. You're often able to switch weapons faster than it takes to reload a weapon—especially if you're using a Sniper Rifle that only holds one round of ammo at a time, for example.

You'll achieve better aiming accuracy if you press the Aim button before pulling the gun's trigger. (In most cases, when you press the Aim button, you'll also zoom in a bit on your enemy.) The process of aiming takes a tiny bit longer, so it's not always practical, based on the dangers you're facing.

Weapon Aiming Tips

Most types of weapons can be shot "from the hip" (meaning you don't accurately aim by pressing the Aim button on your keyboard or controller). You just point the weapon in the direction of your target and pull the trigger. This allows you to attack or defend yourself faster but is less accurate than if you aim first.

Don't Forget to Use Explosives

Grenades and Dynamite, for example, can be tossed through an open window or doorway. If you suspect an enemy is inside of a building, sneak up and peek through a window. Then, toss a few explosive weapons inside. The explosion will typically defeat whoever is inside, plus cause some major damage to the building.

With each new game update that Epic Games introduces, and with each new season of game play, new weapons are often introduced into the game, while others are removed. In some cases, an existing weapon's ratings get tweaked (making it stronger or less powerful).

To stay up-to-date on all of the weapons currently available within *Fortnite: Battle Royale*, and to see the ratings for each weapon, check out any of these independent websites:

- **Fortnite Weapon Stats & Info**—https:// fortnitestats.com/weapons
- **Gamepedia Fortnite Wiki**—https:// fortnite.gamepedia.com/Fortnite_Wiki

- **GameSkinny Fortnite Weapons List**—www.gameskinny.com/9mt22/complete-fortnite-battle-royale-weapons-stats-list

- **Metabomb**—www.metabomb.net/fortnite-battle-royale/gameplay-guides/fortnite-battle-royale-all-weapons-tier-list-with-stats-14

- **Tracker Network (Fortnite)**—https://db.fortnitetracker.com/weapons

Health- and Shield-Related Items

The following chart offers a summary of the popular Health and Shield replenishment items that are typically available on the island. Keep in mind, new items are frequently introduced, while others get vaulted. Be sure you take full advantage of the items currently available in order to help keep your soldier healthy and battle-ready during a match.

As you'll discover, some items get stored within one of your soldier's six main Inventory slots, while others can also be stored within your soldier's inventory, but in a slot found on the Inventory screen to the right of your soldier's Resources. To use them, you must first switch from Combat mode to Building mode, and then select and activate the selected item.

LOOT ITEM	HOW LONG IT TAKES TO USE OR CONSUME	POWERUP BENEFIT	STORAGE LOCATION	MAXIMUM NUMBER YOU CAN CARRY
Apples	Almost Instantly	Increases your soldier's Health meter by 5 points per Apple that's consumed.	Apples must be consumed when and where they're found (which is usually under trees). They cannot be carried and used later.	None
Bananas	Almost Instantly	Increases your soldier's Health meter by 5 points per Banana that's consumed. These items are found mainly in tropical areas.	Bananas must be consumed when and where they're found. They cannot be carried and used later.	None
Bandages	4 seconds	Increases your soldier's Health meter by 15 points.	Requires one backpack inventory slot.	15
Chug Jug	15 seconds	Replenishes your soldier's Health *and* Shield meter to 100.	Requires one backpack inventory slot.	1

LOOT ITEM	HOW LONG IT TAKES TO USE OR CONSUME	POWERUP BENEFIT	STORAGE LOCATION	MAXIMUM NUMBER YOU CAN CARRY
Coconuts	Almost Instantly	Increases your soldier's Health meter by 5 points per Coconut that's consumed. However, if your soldier's Health meter is at 100, his or her Shield meter will receive some replenishment.	Coconuts must be consumed when and where they're found. They cannot be carried and used later.	None
Cozy Campfire	25 seconds	Boosts each soldier's Health HP by 2 points for every second they're standing near the flames for up to 25 seconds. If fully utilized, it boosts a soldier's Health meter by 50 points.	Stored with a soldier's resources, so it's accessed from Building mode, not Combat mode.	Unknown
Med Kits	10 seconds	Replenishes your soldier's Health meter back to 100.	Requires one backpack inventory slot.	3
Mushrooms	Almost instantly	Increases your soldier's Shield meter by 5 points (up to 100).	Mushrooms must be consumed when and where they're found. They cannot be carried and used later.	None
Peppers	Almost Instantly	Increases your soldier's Health meter by 5 points per Pepper that's consumed. Your soldier will also be able to move 20 percent faster for a short time. These items are found mainly in desert areas.	Peppers must be consumed when and where they're found. They cannot be carried and used later.	None

(Continued on next page)

LOOT ITEM	HOW LONG IT TAKES TO USE OR CONSUME	POWERUP BENEFIT	STORAGE LOCATION	MAXIMUM NUMBER YOU CAN CARRY
Shield Potion	5 seconds	Replenishes your soldier's Shield meter by 50 points (up to 100 maximum).	Requires one backpack inventory slot.	2
Slurp Juice	Approximately 2 seconds to consume and 37.5 seconds to achieve its full benefit.	A soldier's Health *and* Shield meter increases by one point (up to 75 points) for every half-second this drink is being consumed.	Requires one backpack inventory slot.	1
Small Shield Potion	2 seconds	Replenishes your soldier's Shield meter by 25 points.	Requires one backpack inventory slot.	10

SECTION 5

FORTNITE: BATTLE ROYALE
RESOURCES

On YouTube (www.youtube.com), Twitch.TV (www.twitch.tv/directory/game/Fortnite), or Facebook Watch (www.facebook.com/watch), in the Search field, enter the search phrase "*Fortnite: Battle Royale*" to discover many game-related channels, live streams, and prerecorded videos that'll help you become a better player.

Also, be sure to check out the following online resources related to *Fortnite: Battle Royale*:

WEBSITE OR YOUTUBE CHANNEL NAME	DESCRIPTION	URL
Best *Fortnite* Settings	Discover the custom game settings used by some of the world's top-rated *Fortnite: Battle Royale* players.	www.bestfortnitesettings.com
Corsair	Consider upgrading your keyboard and mouse to one that's designed specifically for gaming. Corsair is one of several companies that manufacturers keyboards, mice, and headsets specifically for gamers.	www.corsair.com
Epic Game's Official Social Media Accounts for *Fortnite: Battle Royale*	Visit the official Facebook, Twitter, and Instagram Accounts for *Fortnite: Battle Royale*.	Facebook: www.facebook.com/FortniteGame Twitter: https://twitter.com/fortnitegame Instagram: www.instagram.com/fortnite
Fandom's *Fortnite* Wiki	Discover the latest news and strategies related to *Fortnite: Battle Royale*.	http://fortnite.wikia.com/wiki/Fortnite_Wiki
FantasticalGamer	A popular YouTuber who publishes *Fortnite* tutorial videos.	www.youtube.com/user/FantasticalGamer
FBR Insider	The *Fortnite: Battle Royale Insider* website offers game-related news, tips, and strategy videos.	www.fortniteinsider.com
Fortnite Config	An independent website that lists the custom game settings for dozens of top-rated *Fortnite: Battle Royale* players.	https://fortniteconfig.com
Fortnite Gamepedia Wiki	Read up-to-date descriptions of every weapon, loot item, and ammo type available within *Fortnite: Battle Royale.* This Wiki also maintains a comprehensive database of soldier outfits and related items released by Epic Games.	https://fortnite.gamepedia.com/Fortnite_Wiki

(Continued on next page)

WEBSITE OR YOUTUBE CHANNEL NAME	DESCRIPTION	URL
Fortnite Intel	An independent source of news related to *Fortnite: Battle Royale*.	www.fortniteintel.com
Fortnite Scout	Check your personal player stats and analyze your performance using a bunch of colorful graphs and charts. Also check out the stats of other *Fortnite: Battle Royale* players.	www.fortnitescout.com
Fortnite Skins	This independent website maintains a detailed database of all *Fortnite: Battle Royale* outfits and accessory items released by Epic Games.	https://fortniteskins.net
Fortnite Stats & Leaderboard	This is an independent website that allows you to view your own *Fortnite*-related stats or discover the stats from the best players in the world.	https://fortnitestats.com
Fortnite: Battle Royale for Android Mobile Devices	Download *Fortnite: Battle Royale* for your compatible Android-based mobile device.	www.epicgames.com/fortnite/en-US /mobile/android/get-started
Fortnite: Battle Royale Mobile (iOS App Store)	Download *Fortnite: Battle Royale* for your Apple iPhone or iPad.	https://itunes.apple.com/us/app /fortnite/id1261357853
Game Informer Magazine's *Fortnite* Coverage	Discover articles, reviews, and news about *Fortnite: Battle Royale* published by *Game Informer* magazine.	www.gameinformer.com/fortnite
Game Skinny Online Guides	A collection of topic-specific strategy guides related to *Fortnite*.	www.gameskinny.com/tag/fortnite -guides
GameSpot's *Fortnite* Coverage	Check out the news, reviews, and game coverage related to *Fortnite: Battle Royale* that's been published by GameSpot.	www.gamespot.com/fortnite
HyperX Gaming	Manufactures a selection of high-quality gaming keyboards, mice, headsets, and other accessories used by amateur and pro gamers alike. These work on PCs, Macs, and most console-based gaming systems.	www.hyperxgaming.com
IGN Entertainment's *Fortnite* Coverage	Check out all IGN's past and current coverage of *Fortnite*.	www.ign.com/wikis/fortnite

WEBSITE OR YOUTUBE CHANNEL NAME	DESCRIPTION	URL
Jason R. Rich's Websites and Social Media	Learn about additional, unofficial game strategy guides by Jason R. Rich that cover *Fortnite: Battle Royale*, *PUBG*, and *Apex Legends* (each sold separately).	www.JasonRich.com www.GameTipBooks.com Twitter: @JasonRich7 Instagram: @JasonRich7
LazarBeam's YouTube Channel	With more than 11 million subscribers, LazarBeam offers Fortnite: Battle Royale tutorials that are not only informative, but very funny and extremely entertaining. (This Australian gamer seems to be a huge fan of building covered bridges during matches.)	YouTube Channel: http://goo.gl/HXwElg Twitter: https://twitter.com/LazarBeamYT Instagram: www.instagram.com/lazarbeamyt
Microsoft's Xbox One *Fortnite* Website	Learn about and acquire *Fortnite: Battle Royale* if you're an Xbox One gamer.	www.microsoft.com/en-US/store/p/Fortnite-Battle-Royalee/BT5P2X999VH2
MonsterDface YouTube and Twitch.tv Channels	Watch video tutorials and live game streams from an expert *Fortnite* player.	www.youtube.com/user/MonsterdfaceLive www.Twitch.tv/MonsterDface
Ninja	On YouTube and Twitch.tv, check out the live and recorded game streams from Ninja, one of the most highly skilled *Fortnite: Battle Royale* players in the world. His YouTube channel has more than 22 million subscribers.	YouTube: www.youtube.com/user/NinjasHyper Twitch: https://twitch.tv/Ninja
Official Epic Games YouTube Channel for *Fortnite: Battle Royale*	The official *Fortnite: Battle Royale* YouTube channel.	www.youtube.com/user/epicfortnite
Pro Game Guides	This independent website maintains a detailed database of all *Fortnite: Battle Royale* outfits and accessory items released by Epic Games.	https://progameguides.com/fortnite/fortnite-features/fortnite-battle-royale-outfits-skins-cosmetics-list
ProSettings.com	An independent website that lists the custom game settings for top-ranked *Fortnite: Battle Royale* players. This website also recommends optional gaming accessories, such as keyboards, mice, graphics cards, controllers, gaming headsets, and monitors.	www.prosettings.com/game/fortnite www.prosettings.com/best-fortnite-settings

(Continued on next page)

WEBSITE OR YOUTUBE CHANNEL NAME	DESCRIPTION	URL
SCUF Gaming	This company makes high-end, extremely precise, customizable wireless controllers for the console-based gaming systems, including the SCUF Impact controller for the PS4. If you're looking to enhance your reaction times when playing *Fortnite: Battle Royale*, consider upgrading your wireless controller.	www.scufgaming.com
Turtle Beach Corp.	This is one of many companies that make great quality, wired or wireless (Bluetooth) gaming headsets that work with all gaming platforms.	www.turtlebeach.com

Your *Fortnite: Battle Royale* Adventure Continues . . .

There are many battle royale games you can play, like *PUBG* and *Apex Legends*, but there's only one *Fortnite: Battle Royale*! Sure, all of these games share a lot in common, but none have the vast global audience of gamers, and ever-changing game play offerings that Epic Games continues to incorporate into *Fortnite: Battle Royale*.

Not only can you expect dramatic geographic changes on the island with each new gaming season (as well as smaller tweaks with each weekly update or patch), but when it comes to experiencing many different game play modes, *Fortnite: Battle Royale* definitely takes the lead.

With plenty of practice, you might become really good at surviving and potentially winning Solo matches. However, you'll need to broaden your gaming skills when you join with a partner or a squad for a Duos or Squads match. During these matches, you'll need to maintain clear and constant communication with your allies and do whatever you can to help keep them alive as you battle your enemies and strive to achieve #1 Victory Royale.

Keeping your partner alive might mean sharing weapons, ammo, resources, and loot items. It might require you to execute perfectly coordinated attacks, or use one of the game's Revive Vans to keep an ally in the match after they've been defeated.

Of course, while you're working with others, you'll definitely want to watch each other's backs and always use the terrain to your utmost advantage. For example, while one soldier is building or using a Health and/or Shield replenishment item, another soldier can keep their weapon drawn and ready to defend against attacks.

The more you know about the island's terrain, the easier it will be for you and your partner or squad mates to safely find your way around the island and discover all there is to grab along the way. Plus, by watching your fellow gamers at work, you'll likely discover some useful strategies, because everyone has their own gaming style.

Beyond experiencing Solo, Duos, and Squads matches, be sure to check out the other exciting game play modes that *Fortnite: Battle Royale* offers. These different gaming modes offer different challenges, yet all take place on the same mysterious island. Thus, the more you know about the island and its terrain, the bigger advantage you'll have.

Most importantly, if you want to excel when it comes to playing *Fortnite: Battle Royale*, the one additional thing you'll need is plenty of practice! Learn to keep a clear head in the heat of battle, and definitely don't forget to have fun!

Good luck!